# SPORTSMAN'S DIGEST OF HUNTING

## BY HAL SHARP

**BARNES & NOBLE, Inc., New York**
Publishers • Booksellers • Since 1873

*EVERYDAY HANDBOOKS*

©

Copyright 1952, 1953, by General Features Corporation
All rights reserved under International
and Pan-American Copyright Conventions
Published by special arrangement with
Sterling Publishing Company, Inc., Licensee

Reprinted, 1969

L. C. catalogue card number: 54-5726

Manufactured in the United States of America

# EVERYDAY HANDBOOKS

Everyday Handbooks (#201-300) are self-teaching books on academic subjects, skills, and hobbies. The majority of these books sell for $1.25 to $2.25. Many are available in cloth bindings at a higher price.

### ART, BALLET
ART AND ANATOMY, 278
BRIDGMAN'S BOOK OF 100 HANDS, 299
BRIDGMAN'S THE FEMALE FORM, 301
BRIDGMAN'S HEADS, FEATURES AND FACES, 300
BRIDGMAN'S THE HUMAN MACHINE, 303
BRIDGMAN'S LIFE DRAWINGS, 304
GUIDE TO THE BALLET, 282
PAINTINGS OF THE WESTERN WORLD, 281

### BUSINESS, ECONOMICS, LAW
BOOKKEEPING MADE EASY, 235
CAREERS FOR COLLEGE GRADUATES, 283
DICTIONARY OF ECONOMICS, 266
SHORTHAND, 225
TOUCH TYPEWRITING, 229
YOUR INTRODUCTION TO LAW, 286

### EDUCATION
GUIDING YOUR CHILD TOWARD COLLEGE, 295

### ENGLISH, DRAMA
CREATIVE WRITING, 203
ERRORS IN ENGLISH and Ways to Correct Them, 240
EVERYDAY SPEECH: How to Say What You Mean, 239
FAMOUS BOOKS, Ancient and Medieval, 297
FAMOUS BOOKS since 1492, 298
GRAMMAR, RHETORIC AND COMPOSITION, 228
LETTERS FOR ALL OCCASIONS, 237
PLAYBOY OF THE WESTERN WORLD/RIDERS TO THE SEA, 226
PLOT OUTLINES OF 100 BEST NOVELS, 215

### ENGLISH, DRAMA (Continued)
PUBLIC SPEAKING, 207
PUNCTUATE IT RIGHT! 255
SHORT HISTORY OF ENGLISH LITERATURE, 205
SPELL IT RIGHT!, 279
TWELVE WAYS TO BUILD A VOCABULARY, 293
WRITER'S BOOK, 265

### HISTORY, POLITICAL SCIENCE
AMERICAN HISTORY AT A GLANCE, 245
BRIEF HISTORY OF THE WESTERN WORLD, 284
CANADIAN HISTORY AT A GLANCE, 246
DICTIONARY OF AMERICAN POLITICS, 261
THE ESSENTIAL LEFT, 219
READINGS FROM LIBERAL WRITERS, ENGLISH AND FRENCH, 233

### THE HUMANITIES
INTRODUCTION TO THE HUMANITIES: Painting, Sculpture, Architecture, Music and Literature, 277

### LANGUAGES
FRENCH FOR BEGINNERS, 252
GERMAN FOR BEGINNERS, 217
ITALIAN FOR BEGINNERS, 214
RUSSIAN FOR BEGINNERS, 287
SPANISH FOR BEGINNERS, 271

### MATHEMATICS
ARITHMETIC Clear and Simple, 270
MATHEMATICS FOR PRACTICAL USE, 212
SLIDE RULE: How to Use It, 254

## ABOUT THE AUTHOR

Hal Sharp was just four years old in 1918 when his great-grandfather took him on a squirrel hunt in the Ozark Mountains of north-west Arkansas, and he has been hunting ever since. Hal was initiated, too, into the secrets of angling with a "trot" line at the age of four.

When he was nine, he moved with his family to California where he attended school and won a three-year scholarship in art. Later he worked in the animation studios at Hollywood and for three years was a comic book illustrator.

During the Second World War, Hal was a technical engineer and did radar installation drawings for the U. S. Navy. It was at this period in his career that he decided to create the newspaper feature, SPORTSMAN'S DIGEST [from which this book was compiled], to help other sportsmen learn short cuts to the art of hunting and fishing that otherwise might take years of learning.

Nowadays when Hal hits the road with gun or rod, he takes his wife along.

# TABLE OF CONTENTS

Introduction: Hunting ......... 1

1: Small Game and Fowl ......... 7
Rabbit • Squirrel • Coon • Stalking Game Birds • Quail • Grouse • Pheasant • Field Care of Game Birds • Crow

2: Ducks and Geese ......... 33
Blinds • Decoys • Calls • Estimating Shooting Range

3: Big Game ......... 51
Deer • The "Stand" • Stalking • Judging Tracks • Lead Allowance • Field Care • Black Bear • Bighorn Sheep • Bobcat • Care of Trophy Animals • Skinning Big Game • Hanging Big Game • Carriers

4: Trapping ......... 92
Muskrat • Coon • Beaver • Weasel • Fox • Tanning

5: Better Marksmanship ......... 121
How to Avoid Accidents • Offhand Shots • Scope Sights • Waverings • Recoil • Target Practice • Wing Shots • Forward Allowance

6: Rifles and Shotguns ............... 156
Bullets • Sights • "Drop" and "Pitch"

7: Care of Equipment ............... 171
Guns • Ammunition • Outdoor Gear • Binoculars • Clothing

8: Your Dog ............... 192
Touring with a Dog • Food • Boots • Bell • Removing burs, ticks, porcupine quills, skunk odor • Cleaning a Dog's Ears

9: Preparing and Cooking Game ............... 206
Freezer Tips • Eliminating "Wild Taste" • "Aging" Game • Recipes for Rabbit, Squirrel, Quail, Pheasant, Waterfowl, and Venison

10: Woodcraft for the Hunter ....... 221
Using a Compass • Marking a Trail • Distress Signals • Emergency Shelter • Purifying Drinking Water • Quicksand • Camping Sites • Campfires

Index ............... 245

# SPORTSMAN'S DIGEST
OF HUNTING

# HUNTING

This book is for the hunter of popular game animals and birds. The average American's privilege to hunt, regardless of his social or financial status, must be respected and acclaimed, for in some parts of the world hunting is only for the wealthy few.

The average man in such countries cannot know the intense pleasure of matching wits with big or small game nor the thrill of a clean wing shot. Money does not designate a "sportsman" although the term has been used loosely.

Some may wince at the thought of innocent and trusting game birds and animals being slaughtered by the hordes of annual nimrods. These accusers have little understanding of the wild lives of all game and birds.

It is a struggle for birth and survival — a predator or starvation overtakes most game before old age develops into death. Death is violent and sometimes lingering.

In contrast, the sportsman's deliberate aim and fire is by far more humane. It is comparatively quick and serves a purpose at the same time: game crops must be harvested each year to make way for the next year's crop much the same as the farmer's harvesting.

Hunting is one of the earliest instincts of man. It provided his food and clothing and I feel sure that God intended it so. It's true that it's no longer necessary for man's existence to hunt but it is a healthful activity for the body and mind of modern man.

The modern hunter respects and understands conservation. He supports it because he knows that without it game would be completely wiped out eventually. He also knows that official conservation agencies endorse the annual harvest of game. Without this control, birds and beasts would multiply and become nuisances. Or else, as with browsing animals such as deer, they would over-browse their food supply until the range is destroyed. Then starvation would result.

The true sportsman observes local limits of game and will not overshoot his limit. He knows full well that if he should take more than his share and everyone did likewise, the sport would soon be destroyed.

Unfortunately there are many hunters who are not sportsmen in any sense except that they hunt. They should be exposed to public ridicule and their licenses withdrawn, with extreme penalties imposed for their actions. Many states are enacting laws with penalties so extreme as to withdraw forever the privileges of pursuit in a wonderful recreation. The game law violator is a thief and must be treated as such.

I will offer this as a tip right here. Get to know your game officials. They are a fine group and real sportsmen. Many times they will be helpful in locating the best places to hunt.

The privilege of owning and using firearms must be protected. You should go "all-out" to see that your rights shall never be infringed upon by gun cranks who attempt to restrict your ownership or use of firearms. Laws requiring registration, etc., eventually lead to confiscation, as has happened in other parts of the world, when invaders over-ran those countries.

Firearm safety is a "must" for anyone who takes a gun in his hands. Careless handling is inexcusable. Always check the safety on a gun as it is handed to you. If you don't know how it works, ask immediately!

Then ask or have the gun's action opened so that you're sure it is unloaded before handling it. Never point or allow a gun to be pointed at anything you don't mean to kill even if the gun is known to be unloaded! This practice will insure safer handling. If you're not sure of the gun's safe condition, take it to a competent gunsmith for his analysis.

Treat your gun with care, and respect your hunting code. Your gun can cause much sorrow or happiness as you direct it. Don't keep a loaded gun around your house, as you may not always be around to guard it from some careless handler. Ammunition must be kept out of reach of youngsters as well, for without it no injury can result. Be sure of your target before firing and never shoot at anything uncertain in identity.

Be tolerant as a sportsman. The other fellow has his own point of view and much can be learned by keeping your ears and mind open in discussion. Observe the generosity of the landowner who permits you to hunt on his land, by protecting and not damaging his property.

Practice good sportsmanship and you'll be a good sportsman.

There is something of the boy in every man. As one grows older he recalls the happy carefree days when just the simple adventures in woodlands and fields were fulfilling in themselves. He may appreciate the wonders of nature more fully now, but he still finds enjoyment in being afield whether game is in his bag or not. Those days of complete satisfaction of returning with a proud trophy are memorable days to cherish.

It is toward such days of success that this work is directed in hope that the beginner shall learn, in brief accounts, tips that he might otherwise be years in learning. I likewise hope that old-timers will find helpful tips that came to me from old-timers.

Good hunting!

# SMALL GAME AND FOWL

Small game offers the best hunting for the average man because it is accessible locally throughout North America. Most of the millions of hunters began the sport as boys, using .22 rifles and light shotguns or grandfather's old 10 gauge that "kicked like a mule" the first time they used it. Rabbits were then and still are the most popular game. Most big game sportsmen, too, started out by hunting rabbits and squirrels.

Other small game include raccoons, opossum, game birds, various predators and water fowl. In most parts of the country there is some species of small game or predators (such as crows, etc.) to hunt the year round.

The high reproductive rate of cottontails makes it next to impossible to shoot them into extinction. With proper cover and natural food, rabbits will make outstanding gains in spite of the hunters who constantly imperil their lives. Many sportsmen contend that a simple rabbit hunt is as satisfying as a big game hunt. There is no doubt that keen enjoyment is to be had on a crisp fall morning when the frost is on the ground and the game is rabbits. It may be in a field of shocked corn or wheat stubble, a meadow or patch of golden woodland, or it may be among sage-covered foothills. Those who know the pulse-quickening smell of gun smoke in the still air will never forget it.

Many sportsmen relive their early experiences by taking their sons or daughters afield for small game. Thus two things are achieved: pleasant recollections and breaking youngsters into the fold. Here is one of the best ways to teach sportsmanship to a youngster: teach the fundamentals of small game hunting and safety in handling firearms. It's time well spent.

# SMALL GAME AND WATER FOWL SHOT SIZES....

Chapter 1

Small Game and Fowl

Use 7½, 8, or 9 size shot for woodcock, snipe, quail, dove and like size birds.

Pheasant, grouse, rabbit and duck sizes are 5, 6 and 7½'s.

Pass shooting ducks and coot need 4's and 5's.

Squirrel: 4's, 5's or 6's.

Geese, turkey or foxes: BB's, 2's or 4's.

# RABBIT HUNTING FUNDAMENTALS

Chapter 1

Small Game and Fowl

**R**ABBITS FEED HEAVILY AT NIGHT. EARLY MORNING AND LATE AFTERNOON MAY FIND THEM ON THE MOVE. A FEW MAY BE OUT AT NOON BUT NOT TOO FAR FROM A BRUSH PILE OR HOLE.

**I**N SEVERE WEATHER COTTON-TAILS ARE HARD TO FIND; THEY HAVE TO BE "KICKED-OUT." THE DEEPEST HIDERS CAN'T BE MOVED. IMPROVING WEATHER WILL BE "TOPS" FOR GOOD HUNTING!

**H**ARES OR "JACKS" DO NOT HOLE-UP.

# COTTONTAIL TIPS

Chapter 1

Small Game and Fowl

Ideal rabbit cover is criss-crossed with regular paths the rabbits use most often. In dense cover of brush and briars it is difficult to unravel but in weedy clearings you can usually pick the main avenues of entry.

When a rabbit is in such a clearing and is disturbed into leaving, it picks one or more of the paths to use because it can make faster time. The final path it turns into will lead to its home or a brush pile. A wise hunter stations himself at one of these crossings as his partner works toward him.

# RABBIT HUNTING

**Chapter 1**

**Small Game and Fowl**

**A** SHOTGUN IS BEST FOR RABBITS IN MOST AREAS RATHER THAN A .22 RIFLE BECAUSE OF THE DISTANCE A .22 BULLET <u>CAN</u> RICOCHET UPON STRIKING A STONE, TREE BRANCH OR FROZEN GROUND.

**W**ITHOUT THE USE OF A DOG IT'S BEST TO HUNT THE LEE SIDE OF HILLS, RAVINES OR BRUSHY COVER WHEN A COLD WIND IS BLOWING. IN IDEAL COVER, DON'T PASS UP BRUSH PILES, ETC. WITHOUT GIVING EACH A KICK AND TROMPING. RABBITS INVARIABLY RETURN TO THE SPOT WHERE A HOUND HAS JUMPED THEM AND THE HUNTER WHO REMAINS THERE USUALLY GETS A SHOT.

# RABBIT HUNT TIPS

Chapter 1

Small Game and Fowl

A RABBIT USUALLY SEEKS AN UPHILL COURSE TO EVADE PURSUIT BECAUSE HIS LONGER HIND LEGS AFFORD HIM MORE SPEED UPHILL THAN DOWN. THEREFORE, WHENEVER HUNTING IN SUCH AREAS, TWO OR MORE HUNTERS SHOULD SEPARATE, WITH ONE WORKING ALONG THE HILLTOP.

A RABBIT'S SAFETY STRATEGY IS HEADLONG FLIGHT IF DISCOVERED OR IMMOBILITY IF UNSEEN. MOST TIMES HE USES THE LATTER. NEARBY NERVOUS RABBITS MAY EXPOSE THEMSELVES IF THE HUNTER PAUSES FREQUENTLY!

**Chapter 1**

**Small Game and Fowl**

# RABBIT HUNTING TIPS FOR SUCCESS

Heavy brush often offers the most rabbits but the inexperienced hunter will pass up such spots because he can't aim fast enough to shoot as a bunny flits past an opening. The knowing hunter welcomes such targets. <u>Estimating</u> where the rabbit is as it disappears, he fires at the spot in the brush and often gets his rabbit!

On a cold, windy day look for rabbits on the lee or windless side of a hill!

# "WALKING 'EM UP"

**Chapter 1**

**Small Game and Fowl**

CROUCHED LOW IN A CLUMP OF GRASS OR WEEDS, A COTTONTAIL MAY NOT BOUND AWAY UNTIL YOU NEARLY STEP ON HIM. HE PREFERS TO RELY UPON HIS CAMOUFLAGED COLORING TO PREVENT YOUR SEEING HIM. IT USUALLY WORKS IN HIS FAVOR IF YOU PASS NEAR HIM WITHOUT STOPPING BUT IF YOU DO STOP NEARBY WITHOUT SEEING HIM, HE BECOMES NERVOUS AND MAY BOUNCE AWAY.

THIS "WALKING 'EM UP" IS ONE OF THE MOST POPULAR METHODS OF HUNTING BUNNIES WITHOUT A HOUND.

ONE OR MORE RABBIT HUNTERS SHOULD WALK SLOW AND STOP OFTEN WHEN IN A GOOD FIELD.

Chapter 1
Small Game and Fowl

# AVOIDING "RABBIT FEVER"

TULAREMIA, ALSO CALLED "RABBIT FEVER", CAN BE FATAL TO MAN IF THE GERM GETS INTO AN OPEN SCRATCH OR WOUND OF YOUR EXPOSED HANDS. ALL DISEASED MEAT IS SAFE TO EAT IF IT'S COOKED WELL DONE.

WEAR GLOVES OR BEFORE CLEANING RABBITS, WORK A HEAVY SOAP LATHER INTO YOUR HANDS' SKIN. AFTERWARD, ALL DRIED BLOOD OR POSSIBLE CONTAMINATION, BLOCKED BY THE SOAP FILM, FLUSHES OFF IN WASHING YOUR HANDS AGAIN.

DON'T CUT YOURSELF WHILE CLEANING RABBITS! DO NOT SHOOT SLOW, SLUGGISH RABBITS! WAIT 2 OR 3 WEEKS AFTER THE FIRST HEAVY FROST BEFORE HUNTING. COOK ALL RABBITS TO WELL DONE!

# SQUIRREL HUNTING

Chapter 1

Small Game and Fowl

From day-break until just after sun-up is the best time to find squirrels on the move. Late afternoon is the next best time. A crisp clear and quiet morning is best for locating nut crackers whether you may be softly stealing through the woods or sitting motionless and quiet against a tree trunk.

Don't shoot the first one to appear when sitting, wait a bit and others may follow. Upon killing one, leave it lay and you may get more before moving on by remaining still.

# SQUIRREL HUNT TIP

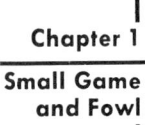

**Chapter 1**

**Small Game and Fowl**

When you are hunting with a friend or two, find a den-tree and hide out of sight near by. Have your pals leave the area. If the squirrels are out, some may try to sneak back to the den-tree after your friends leave and give you some shots. Change places at the next den-trees so each hunter gets in on the shooting.

# SQUIRREL DECOY....

Chapter 1

Small Game and Fowl

Some old time squirrel hunters are very adept at calling up or decoying the bushy tails by rapidly striking two stones together. It may be answered by a chattering squirrel through the woods. Then repeat it once and remain quiet as the squirrel approaches. Commercial callers may be used also.

Listen to squirrels' chatter and practice with this trick.

# UNUSUAL TACTICS FOR SQUIRRELS!

Chapter 1

Small Game and Fowl

Sometimes the unusual pays off in hunting as in anything else. In this case, instead of being quiet and sitting motionless, the idea is to move fast and noisily through the woods, dragging leaves, etc. with your feet but NOT using your voice! Keep looking up into the trees as you go. Stop suddenly and listen. Your unusual noise startles them so that when it is abruptly stopped they may flee without caution. Hurry to head them off with a shotgun before they den-up in a tree.

# MAKE TREED COON SHOW HIMSELF!

**Chapter 1**

Small Game and Fowl

SOMETIMES A COON IS DIFFICULT TO LOCATE IN THE TREE AFTER HOUNDS HAVE TREED IT. HIS CURIOSITY CAN BE AROUSED BY THE IMITATED SOUNDS OF A GOOD COON FIGHT BY THE HUNTERS' SNARLING AND SQUALLING. AS IT BECOMES LOUD AND FIERCE, THE COON WILL EITHER MOVE AROUND SO HE HAS A BETTER VIEW, ENABLING A LIGHT TO SHINE UP HIS EYES IN THE DARKNESS OR HE MAY JUMP OUT OF THE TREE.

Chapter 1

Small Game and Fowl

# STALKING UP TO GAME BIRDS.....

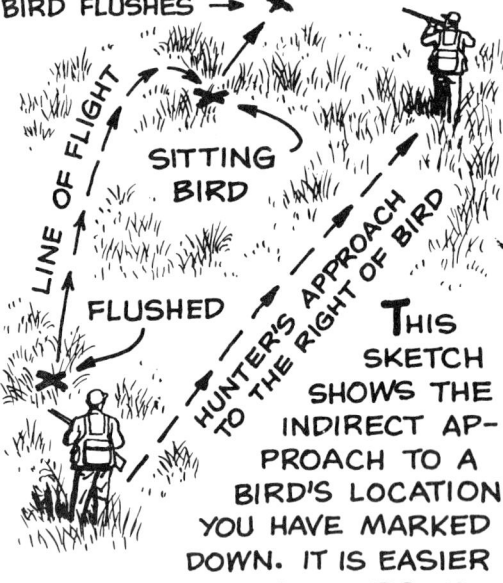

THIS SKETCH SHOWS THE INDIRECT APPROACH TO A BIRD'S LOCATION YOU HAVE MARKED DOWN. IT IS EASIER FOR RIGHT-HAND GUNNERS TO SHOOT TO THE LEFT. LEFT-HAND GUNNERS APPROACH TO THE LEFT (OPPOSITE TO THE SKETCH).

OTHER MERITS OF THIS STALK ARE: EVEN IF YOU ARE IN FULL VIEW TO THE BIRD (ACT UNCONCERNED) IT IS LESS FRIGHTENING AND YOU USUALLY GET CLOSER BEFORE IT FLUSHES. A CROSSING SHOT IS EASIER TO MAKE THAN A STRAIGHTAWAY (FRONTING YOU).

# QUAIL HUNTING TIP

**Chapter 1**

**Small Game and Fowl**

A SCATTERED COVEY OF QUAIL BEGIN CALLING TO REJOIN EACH OTHER AS SOON AS POSSIBLE. WHEN SCATTERED AT NIGHTFALL THE CALLS BEGIN AT ONCE BECAUSE THEY PREFER TO ROOST TOGETHER RATHER THAN ALONE. HOWEVER AS DARKNESS COMES THEY QUIT SO PREDATORS CAN'T FIND THEM. SUCH BIRDS ROOST ALONE. AT DAWN, CALLING RESUMES IN THE <u>SAME</u> AREA WHERE YOU BUSTED THEM LAST NIGHT!

# QUAIL "KNOW-HOW"

Chapter 1

Small Game and Fowl

"**B**IRD FEVER" TO A BIRD SHOOTER IS AS UNNERVING AS "BUCK FEVER" IS TO A DEER HUNTER. IT TAKES A COOL HEAD TO SINGLE OUT ONE BIRD FOR A TARGET WHEN A COVEY FLUSHES ALL AROUND YOU. EVEN THOUGH YOUR DOG HAS POINTED THEM OUT FOR YOU.

**W**HEN CLOSING IN ON A COVEY AHEAD OF POINTING DOGS, HUNTERS SHOULD NOT GET BETWEEN THE BIRDS AND THE NEAREST COVER. BIRDS ALWAYS FLY TO IT REGARDLESS OF HUNTERS, MAKING DIFFICULT HEAD-ON TARGETS.

# GROUSE TRICKS...

BLUE OR DUSKY GROUSE

Chapter 1

Small Game and Fowl

GROUSE, CALLED PARTRIDGE IN SOME AREAS, ARE SO TRUSTING AND TAME IN WILDERNESS SECTIONS THEY ARE REFERRED TO AS "FOOL HENS". NEAR CITIES, YOUNG (NEVER-SHOT-AT) ADULT BIRDS MAY BE TAME AT SEASON'S START BUT WISE-UP <u>FAST</u> AS IT PROGRESSES!

HUNT THEIR FEEDING GROUNDS, BERRIES, WILD GRAPES, ETCETERA, BORDERING THICKETS OR EVERGREENS. THEY MAY SIT SO TIGHTLY THAT HUNTERS WITHOUT DOGS NEARLY STEP ON ONE BEFORE IT FLUSHES TOWARD THICK COVER.

HE HIDES UNDER LOGS, BRUSH, ETC. AS WELL AS IN DEEP WOODS.

# DAILY ROUTINE OF THE GROUSE......

**Chapter 1**

**Small Game and Fowl**

RUFFED GROUSE

A GROUSE OR PARTRIDGE FLIES OFF HIS EVERGREEN ROOST AT SUNUP TO BEGIN HIS STROLL FOR A DRINK, FEEDING AS HE GOES. IF HIS ROOST IS ON A MOUNTAIN, HE MAY FLY QUITE FAR DOWN TO FAVORED FEEDING AREAS. HE PREFERS TO FEED NEAR WATER. THEN HE RESTS IN THE SUN. BY MIDAFTERNOON HE STARTS FEEDING BACK TOWARD THE NIGHT-ROOST.

EAST AND SOUTH HILLSIDES ARE PREFERRED EARLY IN THE DAY, WEST AND NORTH LATER. IN BAD WEATHER THEY STAY IN THICKETS.

# THE EARLY BIRD....

Chapter 1

Small Game and Fowl

**P**HEASANTS MAY BE FOUND ALONG THE ROADSIDES EARLY IN THE MORNING PICKING UP GRAVEL TO GRIND THEIR FOOD WITH LATER IN THE DAY. KNOWING THIS, MANY HUNTERS LEAVE THE CORNFIELDS UNTIL LATER.

**E**ASTERN SLOPES OF MEADOWS OR FIELDS ARE CHOICE ROOST AREAS BECAUSE OF THE EARLY MORNING SUN.

Chapter 1

Small Game and Fowl

# PHEASANT DRIVE

LIMIT THE PHEASANTS' ESCAPE ROUTE TO ONE AREA FOR THE MOST EFFECTIVE DRIVE. ONE OR MORE WAITING HUNTERS SHOULD CONCEAL THEMSELVES BY KNEELING LOW IN WEEDS OR BEHIND BRUSH IN THIS AREA.

AN AUTO MAY BE PARKED TO ONE SIDE OF THE DRIVE AREA NEAR THE FINISH AND A COAT, PERHAPS WITH A CAP, HUNG ON A STAKE ON THE OTHER SIDE (A). THESE SCARE SIDE-ESCAPING BIRDS BACK INTO THE DRIVEN COVER. THE DRIVING HUNTERS ADVANCE SLOWLY, WATCHFUL OF BIRDS SNEAKING BACK. ACTION USUALLY COMES AT DRIVE'S-END.

# FIELD CARE FOR GAME BIRDS.......

Don't carry warm, undrawn birds in a <u>closed</u> <u>game</u> <u>bag</u> or <u>pocket</u>. Drawn birds are carried best hung on a game carrier or tied to rings on boot harness.

All game birds and waterfowl must be drawn quickly or partly digested food and blood clots will taint the flesh and ruin the flavor.

Slit the neck from breast forward and remove gullet and windpipe. Next, cut around vent and slit almost to the breastbone to remove the entrails. Avoid breaking bile sac in the liver. Cut gizzard to remove lining and contents. Wipe insides with a damp cloth. Stuff with dry grass so air circulates through openings.

---

Chapter 1

Small Game and Fowl

**Chapter 1**

**Small Game and Fowl**

# CROW HUNTERS ARE USUALLY WELCOME!

Crow shooting is a good way to make friends among farmers in your local area. Shocked corn and winter wheat become the main winter feed now that insects, rodents, etc. are scarce. The grateful farmer may <u>invite</u> you to return for small game hunting next fall when you need a hunting ground. Crow shooting is sporty, and good for your shooting eye as well!

# CROW HUNTING TIPS: LOCATING A FLOCK

Chapter 1

Small Game and Fowl

A SENTRY CROW WILL ALWAYS BE ON GUARD TO WARN THE FLOCK WHEN ANY DANGER APPEARS, WITH 3 OR 4 STACCATO CRIES REPEATED AT SHORT INTERVALS THE ALARM SIGNAL.

DON'T STOP YOUR CAR ON THE SPOT BUT CONTINUE UNTIL OUT OF SIGHT. HIDE CAR OR CIRCLE SOME DISTANCE AWAY FROM IT AND SECRETE YOURSELF IN THE BEST COVER AT HAND. USING A CALL, SOUND THE ALARM SIGNAL. ANSWERING CROWS COME FAST AS YOUR CALL GROWS IN VOLUME AND EXCITEMENT!

# BEST CROW BAIT

**Chapter 1**

**Small Game and Fowl**

THE GREAT HORNED OWL IS A CROW'S HATED ENEMY.

IN SOME AREAS IT IS LEGAL TO USE A LIVE OWL BUT AN IMITATION MAY BE USED FOR A DECOY. STAKE IT OUT IN OPEN VIEW OF A CROW FLYWAY, NEAR BRUSH OR A BRUSH BLIND THAT HIDES YOU. WHEN A FLIGHT IS SIGHTED, GIVE THE ALARM CALL, THREE OR FOUR HARSH CRIES AND FOLLOW UP SOUNDING CALL LIKE AN ANGRY CROW TELLING AN ENEMY OFF!

CROWS DIVE-ATTACK THE OWL.

# DUCK BLIND TIPS

PINTAIL DUCK

Chapter 2

Ducks and Geese

Puddle ducks such as baldpates, blacks, floridas, mallards, pintails, teal etc. come in to ponds, puddles and sloughs located among trees. Diving ducks, the bufflehead, canvasback, eiders, golden-eyes, etc. prefer more open water. Locate your blind according to the type of ducks you'll have.

Ducks come in and take off against the wind, so build the blind so that the prevailing wind will be on your back as you face the decoy area. The incoming ducks will be flying directly toward or in front of you.

Chapter 2

Ducks and Geese

# MAKE A PORTABLE GRASS BLIND......

1/2" X 1 3/4" LATH

Use any length of chicken wire about 4 ft. wide. Cut laths to the same length. Use small nails to fix the wire to laths. Space laths about 18 inches apart. The completed job can be rolled and used many times.

To use, weave grass, rushes, etc. upright between wires.

# BUILDING A WATER-FOWL GRASS BLIND

DRIVEN CORNER POSTS

GROUND

REMOVABLE SLATTED FLOORING FITS INSIDE TO KEEP FEET OFF GROUND.

FILL IN BE-TWEEN CROSS BARS WITH VARIED LENGTHS OF GRASS, TULES, ETC.

Chapter 2

Ducks and Geese

Cross pieces of weather-beaten lumber are nailed to the corner posts. Brown or green canvas (as near as possible to the color of the natural grass, etc. used) may be fixed inside the blind to break the wind. Gather grass from the area and replace when it begins to change in color to its surroundings.

# NATURAL BLINDS FOR DUCK HUNTERS

**Chapter 2**
**Ducks and Geese**

Rocks, trees, stumps, etc. can serve for blinds as well as the various grasses. Wear grayish clothing. It is less conspicuous than yellowed browns which can be seen farther away.

As soon as you see ducks approaching in the distance, kneel beside your blind. Keep your face down, otherwise it shows up from the sky as an alarm. Hold gun close, pointed straight up to lessen reflected sunlight glints.

# A SIMPLE BLIND FOR DUCK HUNTING

**Chapter 2**

Ducks and Geese

CHOICE DUCK SHOOTING LOCATIONS OFTEN HAVE NO NATURAL COVER WITHIN GUN RANGE TO HIDE GUNNERS. REMEDY THIS BY CUTTING A SMALL OAK (OR OTHER LEAFY) SAPLING FOR AN UMBRELLA-LIKE COVER. IT SCREENS YOU FROM ABOVE AS YOU SUPPORT IT AND THE GUN WITH ONE HAND, AS SHOWN ABOVE. WHEN DUCKS ARE WITHIN RANGE, BRUSH THE SCREEN ASIDE TO SHOOT.

Chapter 2
Ducks and Geese

# A ONE MAN BARREL PIT BLIND FOR SAND BAR OR FIELD.......

SHELL SHELF

DRILL HOLES FOR DRAINAGE IN BARREL BOTTOM

SEAT ROCKS

**P**ICK THE LARGEST WATER TIGHT WOODEN BARREL YOU CAN FIND WHICH WILL FIT YOU. DIG A HOLE AND PLACE ROCKS ON THE BOTTOM (TO HELP KEEP IT DRY). DRILL BOTTOM HOLES, FIX SEAT AND SHELF BEFORE BARREL IS LOWERED IN PLACE. A COVER KEEPS RAIN OUT WHEN NOT IN USE.

## HERE IS ONE TO KEEP YOU WARM ON A COLD "STAND"

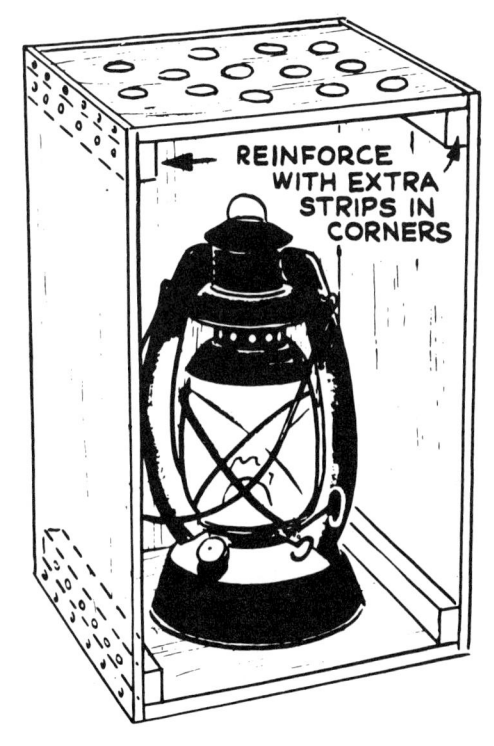

REINFORCE WITH EXTRA STRIPS IN CORNERS

Chapter 2

Ducks and Geese

**It's a strong wooden box, sturdy enough to sit on and larger than an old-fashioned kerosene barn lantern. Bore holes in one end. Solid comfort in a 'blind' or fishing boat and downwind deer stand.**

# NATURAL LOOKING DECOYS PAY OFF...

Chapter 2

Ducks and Geese

**S**ELECT THE MOST LIFE-LIKE DECOYS OF THE SPECIES YOU WANT TO DECOY. BEWARE OF THE CHEAP, CRUDE BLOCKS. BUY THE BEST YOU CAN. PROFESSIONAL HAND-MADE DECOYS ARE BEST IF YOU DON'T WANT TO GO HOME WITH AN EMPTY BAG.

**R**EMOVE ANY DECOYS FROM THE RIG THAT DO NOT FLOAT NATURALLY AND ARE OBVIOUS FAKES TO THE INCOMING BIRDS.

**I**F ICE IS LIKELY TO FORM ON THE DECOYS, RUB A BIT OF VASELINE ON THOSE AREAS TO BE PROTECTED.

# HOW MANY DECOYS FOR A GOOD RIG ?

CLEAR SPACE FOR IN-COMING DUCKS

STRAGGLER DECOY APPEARS TO BE SWIMMING TO JOIN OTHERS IN A "V" FORMATION

Chapter 2

Ducks and Geese

**M**ALLARDS OR OTHER PUDDLE DUCKS MAY ONLY NEED FROM SIX TO EIGHTEEN DECOYS ON STREAMS OR SMALL BODIES OF WATER. DON'T CROWD THESE DECOYS TOGETHER AS THIS INDICATES TO LIVE DUCKS THAT THEY ARE PREPARING TO TAKE FLIGHT OR ARE JUST LOOKING THINGS OVER. MEANING: INSECURITY AT PRESENT.

**D**IVER DUCKS IN MORE OPEN WATER DECOY BEST TO CLOSER FORMATIONS OF MANY DECOYS.

**S**HOWN ABOVE IS A GOOD SIMPLE FORMATION TO USE.

# DUCK DECOY TRICKS

**Chapter 2**
**Ducks and Geese**

## A BLACK DUCK DECOY

**B**LACK DUCKS ARE PERHAPS THE MOST SUSPICIOUS AND CRITICAL OF THE PUDDLE OR MARSH DUCKS. A FEW GOOSE DECOYS MIXED IN A STOOL OF BLACKS AND MALLARD BLOCKS WILL MAKE THE BLACKS LESS WARY.

**S**ET A FEW GOOSE DECOYS UPWIND OR UPSTREAM SEPARATED FROM THE DUCK DECOYS ABOUT 20 FEET.

**P**LACE THE SET SO THE BOAT OR BLIND IS DOWNWIND FROM IT WITH THE SUN IN THE EYES OF THE INCOMING DUCKS.

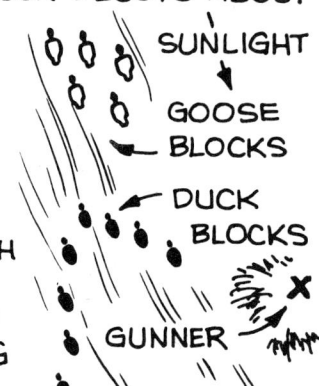

SUNLIGHT
GOOSE BLOCKS
DUCK BLOCKS
GUNNER

# WATERFOWL DECOY TIPS FOR REALISM!

**Chapter 2**

Ducks and Geese

Cut off the wings of the ducks or geese you shoot and nail them onto the decoys in a natural folded position. They will last for the season and will add appeal to your rig.

Different attitudes among the decoys, such as feeding and resting gives them a more realistic look.

Old decoys may be refinished after sanding off old paint. Fill shot holes and cracks with plastic wood. Apply linseed oil, let it dry. Special decoy paint kits are available. Scratch feather outlines in the fresh paint.

Chapter 2
Ducks and Geese

# USING A DUCK CALL

When ducks acknowledge your call and set their wings to glide in to your decoys, you know you've given a call...

Lesser Scaup

...they like, so continue the same call. If they won't come in, try a different call.

Don't take your eyes off the ducks unless they're directly above when calling.

The "highball" call, "quack, quack, quack-quack-quack!" may attract passing ducks. If so, discontinue calling.

High pitched calls work best in timbered areas. Use the low pitch in more open areas. Plead with all calls.

# "HOW FAR?" RANGE ESTIMATED QUICKLY WITH THIS SKETCH!

Chapter 2

Ducks and Geese

MALLARD DUCK SIZE AT 30 YDS.

45 YDS.

60 YDS.

**H**OLD THE MUZZLE OF YOUR SHOTGUN DIRECTLY UNDER EACH DUCK SO THAT YOU MAY EASILY FIX RELATIVE SIZE FOR LATER USE. THIS ALSO APPLIES TO ALL DUCK-SIZE BIRDS.

**E**XTREME RANGE FOR 12 GUAGE 2 3/4 IN. SHELL WITH 1 1/4 OZ. SHOT IS 60 YDS.

**B**EYOND 60 YDS., PASS IT BY!

# JUDGING THE RANGE OF INCOMING DUCKS

Chapter 2

Ducks and Geese

When shooting over decoys you will know the ducks are within range if they compare in size to the decoys. Most decoys are made larger than life-size for better visibility but remember that a <u>flying</u> duck <u>looks</u> larger because it is active.

When a permanent blind is used, markers can be set up 40 yards away to establish the range. Shooting beyond this range usually results in cripples that swim away.

# WHEN IS A DUCK IN SHOOTING RANGE?

**Chapter 2**

**Ducks and Geese**

Generally reliable is the rule that when a duck's colors can be <u>clearly</u> seen, the range is about 30 to 35 yards.

Inexperienced duck hunters are tempted to shoot too soon at passing ducks. This often causes the ducks to flare away, thereby lessening opportunities for better shots.

You'll score more at 35 yds!

# "JUMP SHOOTING" DUCK TIPS..........

Chapter 2

Ducks and Geese

**A** POSSIBLE PLAN OF COVERING SMALL WINDING STREAMS SHOWING HOW IMPORTANT BENDS OF THE STREAM MAY BE COVERED. DUCKS AT "X" MAY BE MISSED BECAUSE OF SLIGHT STREAM DEVIATIONS.

**A**PPROACH EACH BEND SLOWLY AND QUIETLY. THESE DUCKS RISE OR JUMP VERTICALLY FAST. FIRE AS THE DUCKS LEVEL OFF.

# DUCK HUNTER'S SAFE BOAT TIPS

**Chapter 2**

Ducks and Geese

Distribute heavy gear evenly so that it is not all at either end for better handling and seaworthiness. Keep weight low in the bottom for best balance, but don't lay guns there. Water may damage them or they might be accidentally discharged! Guns are best kept handily forward.

Do not stand up to shoot. The recoil may throw you off balance and into icy water.

Open water is always rougher than sheltered water. If it is rough, don't proceed!

**Chapter 2**

**Ducks and Geese**

# PIT BLIND GOOSE SHOOTING TIPS....

Select a field where geese come in to feed or pass over enroute to other grain fields.

With the owner's permission, return at night to dig a pit to suit your needs. It should be deep enough to hide within. Carry the fresh dug earth away and scatter straw around pit before leaving.

Return before dawn with a few stake-out decoys for your shooting. When done shooting, fill pit. Use a different location each day!

# BIG GAME

Big game is hunted throughout most of North America. The western and northern areas offer more variety of big game, but smaller big game is found in most of the other sections. Usually fair hunting is to be had in a nearby state, if not in your own. Hunters are aiming for big game in increasing numbers every year.

An annual hunt can be inexpensive where game is nearby. Deer are found in most states and are the most popular quarry. Quite often it is possible to drive from the city and hunt for a day, returning the same night. The most desirable hunt is for the season, from a base camp located off the beaten path. The camp may be luxurious or a simple tarp lean-to or a tent to suit your pocket book. In many cases, a tent is the best because you can locate closer to the best hunting areas.

**Chapter 3**

**Big Game**

# LEAVE THEM ALONE!

Every year, numbers of people find unattended fawns and want to help them. Thinking the doe has abandoned the fawn, it is taken home. Invariably, the fawn should be left alone because the doe is usually driven away by your approach and is in hiding nearby, perhaps watching you.

The law in most cases prohibits molesting wildlife, nests, etc. because the mother will return.

# TIP-OFF SOUNDS TO AID A HUNTER!

**Chapter 3**

**Big Game**

A SQUIRREL'S VEHEMENT SCOLDING IS HEARD ANYTIME HIS DOMAIN IS TRESPASSED UPON. THE INTRUDER MAY BE A MAN BUT MOST OFTEN IT'S OTHER WILDLIFE! JAY BIRDS REACT IN THE SAME MANNER. THEREFORE THESE ALARMERS CAN AID YOU IN HUNTING.

IF YOU REMAIN QUIET THE SCOLDING USUALLY STOPS. IF YOU HAVE NOT DISTURBED A SQUIRREL AND THEN YOU SUDDENLY HEAR ONE SCOLDING, IT MAY SIGNIFY THAT GAME IS NEARBY. SCOLDING IS USUALLY SHORT TO FAMILIAR INTRUDERS.

OTHER ALARMERS ARE CROWS, HAWKS, BEAVERS, ETCETERA.

Chapter 3
Big Game

# OLD DEER HUNTERS' TRICKS

Some of these are still in use.

Avoid light-colored clothing as it is more easily seen in motion.

A growth of beard or deep tan on a man's face is less conspicuous.

Hide yourself as much as possible. Some climb rocks or trees and remain motionless.

Avoid using shaving lotion, hair tonic or scented soap.

Rub old clothes with cedar oil and hang in a barn before wearing. Rub scent glands of a fresh kill on your boots.

# GET AN EARLY START

Chapter 3

Big Game

It's best to start hunting in the first light of morning. That is when your game is feeding and on the move. Often you may have a hike to the best feeding areas and you want to **be** there early to meet your quarry. Therefore you need a quick breakfast.

Make some sandwiches and fill a vacuum bottle with hot coffee before retiring at night. It will serve for a starter in the morning and you won't be delayed by building a fire and cooking. Your camp is quieter and aromas won't alarm the game.

Chapter 3

Big Game

# HUNTING FROM A "STAND" PAYS OFF!

**R**EMAIN MOTIONLESS!

**F**IND A SADDLE ON A RIDGE THAT GAME USE TO PASS THROUGH FROM ONE VALLEY TO ANOTHER. SEAT YOURSELF OR STAND DOWN WIND FROM THE PASSING TRAIL SO THAT YOU HAVE A GOOD VIEW. DON'T SILHOUETTE YOURSELF AGAINST THE SKY BUT KEEP A TREE OR STUMP BEHIND YOU.

**E**ARLY TO MID-MORNING IS THE BEST TIME FOR A STAND IF YOU DON'T HAVE DRIVERS TO KEEP THE GAME MOVING. GAME SUCH AS DEER ARE MOVING THEN BUT WILL BED DOWN LATER. THEN IS THE TIME FOR STILL HUNTING.

**T**RY IT THE FIRST FEW DAYS!

# HIDE AND LET THE GAME COME TO YOU

Chapter 3

Big Game

Pick a tree trunk, trees or rocks for a back-drop BEHIND you so you are not silhouetted. A screen of boughs in front may be used but are not necessary IF you remain immobile.

A moving or feeding deer moves into the wind, so station yourself so the wind will not betray your position to the game.

One plan is shown above.

# PICK YOUR SHOTS IN TIMBER.........

**Chapter 3**

**Big Game**

If the timber or heavy brush obscures the deer most of the time and prevents maintaining a proper lead, pick an opening through which you will be able to shoot as the deer bounds past. As soon as its head appears, pull the trigger while aiming shoulder high in the opening's center.

You'll get your game and not just score on a tree!

# HALF OF THE FUN OF HUNTING IS STALKING!

**Chapter 3**

**Big Game**

Mountains, desert, plains or woodland hunting, all require a successful stalk of one kind or another. You must conceal your movements as much as possible and move soundlessly against the breezes, whether following a fresh track or just huntin'. A true woodsman covers less than four miles a day in speed! You'll see more, become less tired and, barring "buck fever," get better shots! What's more, the satisfaction is greater!

**Chapter 3**

**Big Game**

# Stalking Big Game

Direction of air currents helps locate game. Deer move down to water at dark and before sunrise. Unless a stiff wind is blowing, air currents are likely to be moving downward at night.

When daylight comes, the breezes turn uphill again. Now the deer moves to the higher ground to scent any danger moving upwind.

Hunt from the ridges down during the sun shine hours, or <u>if</u> the sun is hidden by clouds, and is cloudy most of the time, hunt from the valleys upward to the ridges. When possible, hunt <u>against</u> the wind!

# UP CANYON DRIVE PLAN FOR DEER

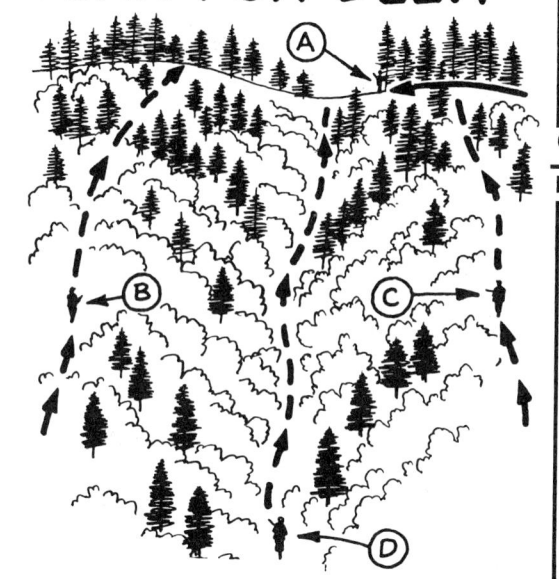

Chapter 3
Big Game

Hunter on a stand (A) is allowed ample time to conceal himself at saddle on ridge at canyon's head after a side approach along main ridge. Hunters (B) and (C) start up the canyon's side slopes below their ridges to be ahead of hunter (D) who is last to start. Hunter-drivers work ahead quietly. Thus driven deer move out slower than they would otherwise.

# GAME IS HARD TO FIND WHEN THE WIND BLOWS!

**Chapter 3**
**Big Game**

WILD GAME ANIMALS DO NOT LIKE WIND ANY MORE THAN YOU DO. HEAVY WIND DRIVES GAME TO THE LEEWARD HILLSIDES AND PROTECTED VALLEYS OR DEEP WOODS AND CEDAR SWAMPS. HERE THEY REMAIN BESIDE WINDFALLS UNTIL THE WEATHER CHANGES. IF TREES ARE LIABLE TO CRASH, EVEN BIG GAME WILL MOVE INTO CLEARINGS. RESTLESS GAME CANNOT DETECT DANGER SOUNDS ABOVE THE HOWLING WINDS.

SMALL GAME, RABBITS, SQUIRRELS, ETC. HOLE-UP AND PHEASANTS WILL SEEK FENCE-ROWS, BRUSH-PILES, ETC. DUCKS MOVE ABOUT BEST BECAUSE THEY ARE SEEKING A QUIET SPOT.

# HOW TO JUDGE A FRESH TRACK....

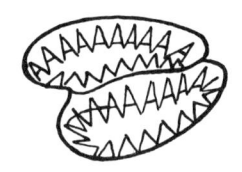

**Chapter 3**
**Big Game**

If FROST CRYSTALS ARE FORMED IN THE TRACK OF ANY GAME, AFTER A NIGHT OF HEAVY FROST, THE TRACK WAS MADE BEFORE THE FROST. BUT IF NO FROST CRYSTALS ARE IN THE TRACK AND FROST IS PRESENT, IT'S FRESH!

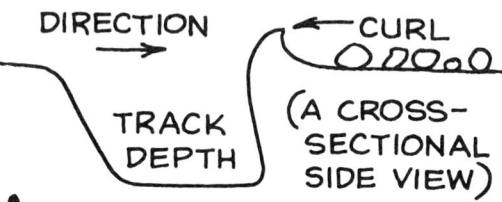

DIRECTION → ← CURL

TRACK DEPTH (A CROSS-SECTIONAL SIDE VIEW)

A FRESH TRACK IN SNOW WILL HAVE A CRISP CURL AND PARTICLES KICKED OUT IN FRONT OF IT. IT IS NOT FRESH WHEN EVAPORATION HAS DULLED THIS CRISPNESS AFTER A FEW HOURS.

When THE SUN DRIES THE DEW OR FROST FROM A DIRT TRACK, ITS EDGES CRUMBLE.

A GOOD HUNTER KNOWS TRACKS!

# TRACKING DEER -BUCK OR DOE?-

*Chapter 3*
*Big Game*

A DOE OR YOUNG BUCK WALKS WITH THE HOOF POINTED STRAIGHT AHEAD. THE TRACKS ARE CLOSE TO AN IMAGINARY CENTER LINE OR YOU CAN DRAW ONE ON THE GROUND BETWEEN THEM WITH A STICK. SMALLER HIND HOOF OVERLAPS SLIGHTLY AHEAD OF THE FRONT HOOF TRACK.

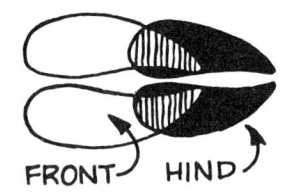

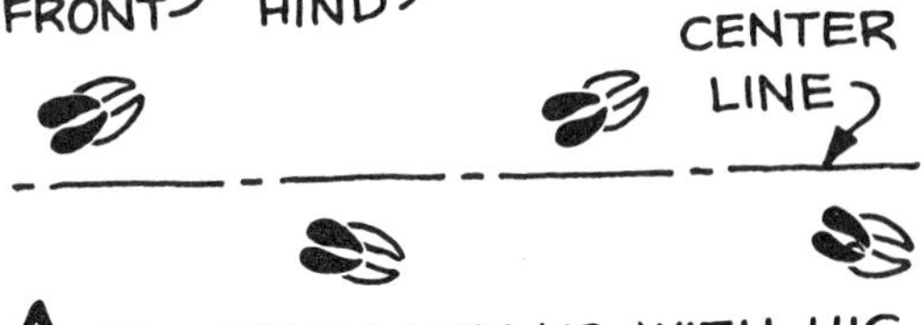

A BIG BUCK WALKS WITH HIS HOOFS POINTED SLIGHTLY OUTWARD AND FARTHER AWAY FROM THE CENTER LINE. SMALLER HIND TRACK REACHES SHORT OF HIS FRONT TRACK.

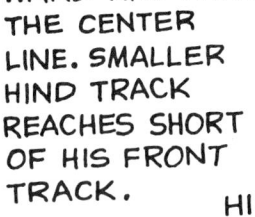

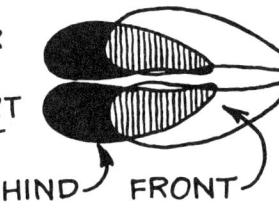

# TRACKING DEER
# -IS IT WOUNDED?-

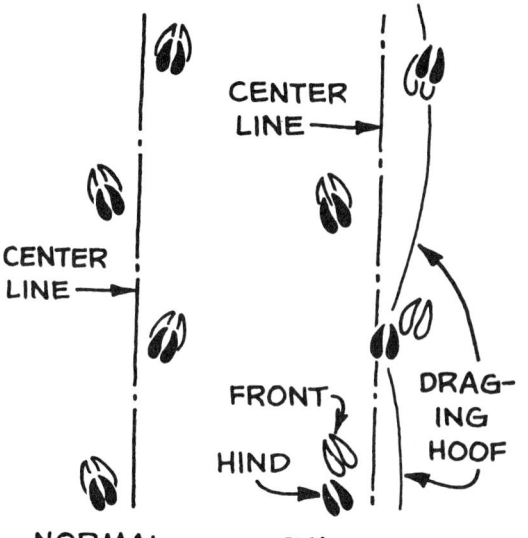

Chapter 3

Big Game

**NORMAL BUCK WALKING**

**STAGGERING TRACKS OF A WOUNDED BUCK**

- CENTER LINE
- CENTER LINE
- FRONT
- HIND
- DRAGING HOOF

A WOUNDED BUCK'S TRACK VARIES ON AND WIDELY OFF A CENTER LINE. ONE OR ALL OF HIS HOOFS MAY DRAG ERRATICALLY. THE NORMAL PLACEMENT OF HIS SMALL HIND HOOF TO OVERLAP, SLIGHTLY BEHIND, HIS FRONT TRACK MAY VARY IN AN IRREGULAR MANNER WHEN A BUCK IS HARD HIT. <u>NEVER</u> LEAVE THE TRAIL OF A WOUNDED DEER.

# LEAD ALLOWANCE FOR BIG GAME....

**Chapter 3**
**Big Game**

SHOOT AHEAD OF A FAST-MOVING DEER

Some riflemen believe that it isn't necessary to maintain a lead ahead of big game with a high velocity rifle. They are wrong if the game is moving fast.

Deer trot at 10 to 20 M.P.H. when startled and under full speed, perhaps 40 M.P.H. If a crossing deer's speed at 100 yds. is 24 M.P.H. (36 ft. per sec.), the deer will move 4 ft. while your bullet moves to it at 2,700 ft. per sec. (the muzzle velocity of the average deer load cartridge.)

Lead varies with the speed!

# DEER'S VITAL AREAS

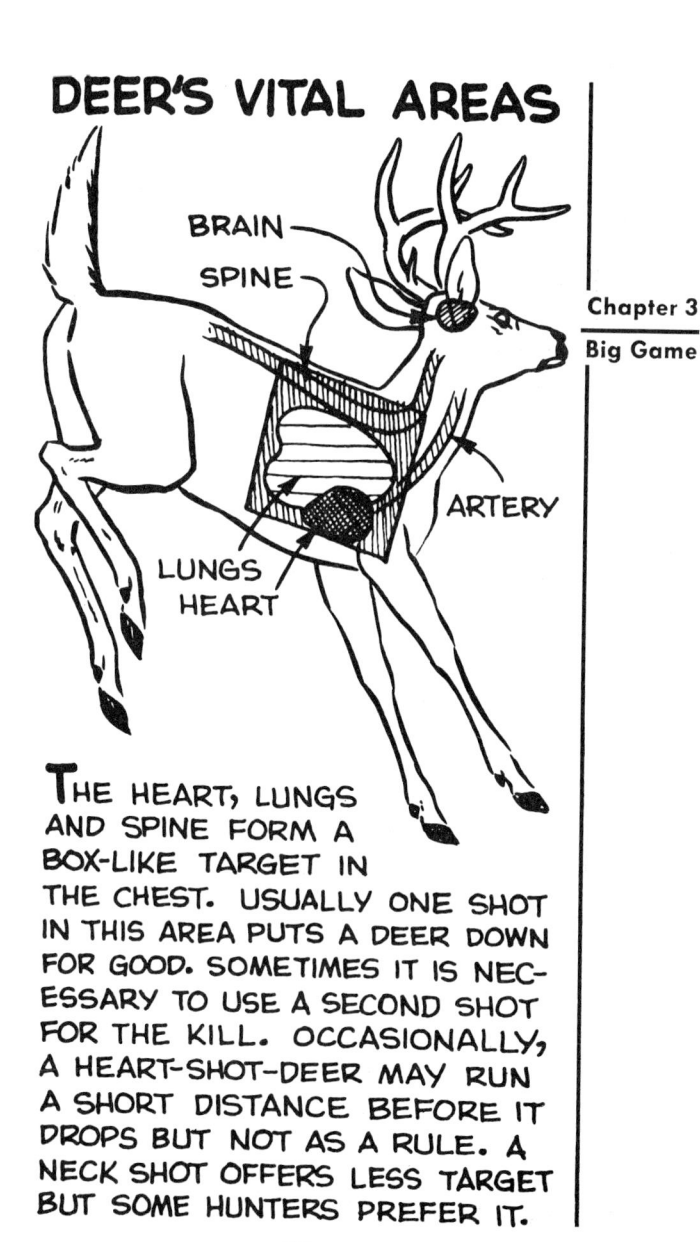

BRAIN
SPINE
ARTERY
LUNGS
HEART

Chapter 3

Big Game

THE HEART, LUNGS AND SPINE FORM A BOX-LIKE TARGET IN THE CHEST. USUALLY ONE SHOT IN THIS AREA PUTS A DEER DOWN FOR GOOD. SOMETIMES IT IS NECESSARY TO USE A SECOND SHOT FOR THE KILL. OCCASIONALLY, A HEART-SHOT-DEER MAY RUN A SHORT DISTANCE BEFORE IT DROPS BUT NOT AS A RULE. A NECK SHOT OFFERS LESS TARGET BUT SOME HUNTERS PREFER IT.

# BE SURE IT'S DEAD!

Chapter 3
Big Game

Each fall there are new stories of how some careless deer or other big game hunter has been injured by the supposed dead game!

After you THINK the game is dead, with your gun ready in one hand, use a LONG stick in the other to brush the game's eyes. The game usually reacts if it still lives! Hold on to your gun if you're not sure it is dead!

# THE METATARSAL GLANDS OF DEER

These musk glands must be sliced off at once after a kill to prevent their fluid secreting into the meat. One gland is located on the outside of each hind leg (as shown) and another is found above it on the inner side. Glands are covered with raised tufts of hair.

Mule deer glands Ⓐ are largest, 3 to 6 in. long. White-tail deer's Ⓑ are smallest, about 1 inch. Blacktail deer Ⓒ is from 1 to 3 in. long. Rinse hands before continuing to dress out to avoid tainting meat.

Chapter 3
Big Game

Chapter 3
Big Game

# FIELD DRESSING DEER, ETC.

RINSE YOUR HANDS AFTER ① AND ②

PROP DEER ON ITS BACK, HEAD UPHILL ON A GENTLE SLOPE. SLICE OFF THE METATARSAL GLANDS ① ON THE LOWER LEGS. CUT AROUND GENITALS ② AND TIE OFF WITH A STRONG CORD. MAKE A CUT AROUND VENT 2" DEEP ③. PULL OUT GUT AND TIE IT OFF ④. KNIFE THROUGH TO THE AITCHBONE ⑤, CUTTING IT WITH KNIFE OR SMALL AXE. SPLIT BELLY TO RIBS ⑥, GUIDING KNIFE BETWEEN 2 FINGERS OF OPPOSITE HAND. SPLIT RIBS ⑦. STOP AT DOTTED LINE IF HEAD'S A TROPHY. IF NOT, OPEN NECK TO HEAD ⑧ TO REMOVE GULLET. CUT DIAPHRAM FREE. ROLL INSIDES OUT.

# A BLOOD-PROOF BAG FOR DEER HUNTERS

A CLEAN SALT, SUGAR OR FLOUR BAG WILL SERVE. OR MAKE ONE OUT OF MUSLIN OR SIMILAR MATERIAL ABOUT 8" BY 16" IN SIZE. RUB WAX ON THE OUTSIDE THEN PRESS IT IN WITH A WARMED IRON.

A DRAW-STRING TOP IS HANDY OR TWIST THE TOP AND TIE IT INTO A KNOT FOR A CLOSURE.

IT'S USED TO CARRY THE HEART AND LIVER BACK TO CAMP. TIED TO YOUR BELT IT LEAVES THE HANDS FREE.

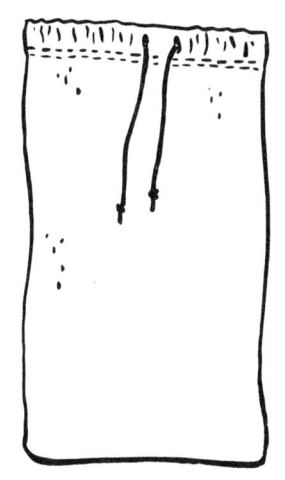

Chapter 3
Big Game

Chapter 3
Big Game

# HUNTING BLACK BEAR

As slow as this critter looks, it can easily outrun any man! He relies upon his sense of smell and keen hearing. Upon scenting a man, he will usually run the other way. His usual pace, unless disturbed, is slow and silent.

A bear should be approached or stalked from uphill if possible. Two good reasons are, ① in mountainous bear country, the wind or breeze is uphill usually— ② wounded bear moves faster <u>downhill</u>!

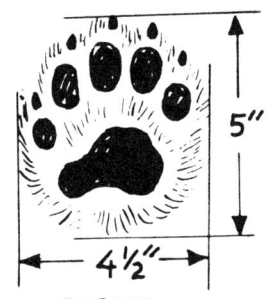

RIGHT FORE FOOT (5" × 4½")

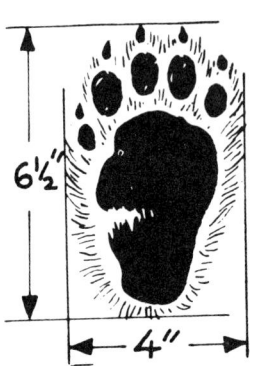

RIGHT HIND FOOT (6½" × 4")

# BIGHORN SHEEP....

**Chapter 3**
Big Game

This trophy is considered by many big game hunters the most prized of all North American game! They range from Sonora, Mex. and Lower California to Alaska. Sheep are hunted in the United States only in Wyoming. Alaska and Western Canada furnish the best hunting. In Mexico the hunting is fair.

**90%** of the successful hunt is due to the careful stalk which demands good binoculars for spotting the game and only 10% for shooting!

# BOBCAT HUNTING...

**Chapter 3**

**Big Game**

For this sport one or more hounds are essential. If you have none, local game officials may know a cat hunter who can arrange a hunt with hounds. It's a thrilling winter hunt and cats inhabit most rural areas in North America!

Maps showing swamps, streams and remote roads should be studied. A hounded cat travels in circles. The smaller the swamp, the smaller the circles. A narrow neck connecting two swamps or a dividing road is a good place for a "stand." Motionless, you may get a shot as the cat passes in front of the hounds.

# A SINGLE HUNTER HUNTING BOBCATS

**Chapter 3**
**Big Game**

A BOBCAT'S TRACK IS SIMILAR TO A HOUSE CAT'S BUT LARGER. IN WALKING, A CAT'S CLAWS ARE WITHDRAWN SO THEY DON'T APPEAR IN THE TRACK.

THE WOODS-WISE HUNTER WHO FOLLOWS A COLD TRACK WITH A SLOW, QUIET HOUND ON A LEASH BEFORE HIM MAY OVERTAKE THE CAT WHO IS BEDDED FOR THE DAY BY SNEAKING UP ON HIM. INTENTLY WATCHING AHEAD, THE HUNTER MAY GET A SHOT AS THE CAT LEAVES ITS BED. A SHOTGUN FIRING BB'S OR NUMBER 2 SHOT IS THE BEST FOR SUCH HUNTING. START EARLY AND PREPARE FOR A LONG HIKE.

Chapter 3
Big Game

# BOBCAT HUNTING METHODS

RIGHT HIND TRACK

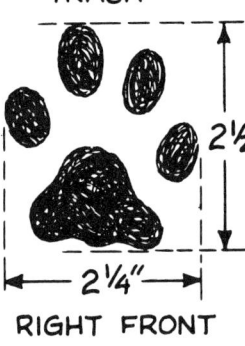

2½"

← 2¼" →

RIGHT FRONT TRACK

A FAST PACK OF FOXHOUNDS WILL CHASE A CAT FOR HOURS IN BRUSHY COVER OF THE SOUTH EASTERN STATES. THE GUNNERS MAY SELECT A "STAND" IN AN OPENING TO WAIT WITH A SHOTGUN FOR A SHOT AS THE CAT CIRCLES BACK IN FRONT OF THE DOGS--OR THE DOGS MAY KILL THE CAT WHEN IT COMES TO BAY. IN THE SOUTH, ON OCCASION, IT WILL TREE— BUT IN THE WEST, WHEN HARD PUSHED, IT TREES READILY.

DUE TO HEAVY SNOWS OF THE NORTH, ONLY TWO DOGS AND ONE HUNTER CAN FORCE THE BOUNDING BUT TIRING CAT TO TREE.

# IS IT NECESSARY TO "BLEED" A TROPHY?

Chapter 3

Big Game

Today's modern bullets are constructed to open up according to the type of game intended for it. When the correct bullet is used it should not be necessary to cut a neck artery for further bleeding. The damaging bullet has usually torn a large hole that provides for bleeding. On-the-spot dressing of deer removes the blood also.

# ANTLERED TROPHY

**Chapter 3**

**Big Game**

If a delay to the taxidermist is expected proceed as follows: cut skin at top of shoulder, etc. as shown. Allow extra around the chest. Pull skin inside out at ear base and cut free. Work carefully around eyes, nose and mouth. "Flesh" skin and salt well. Roll up for a day, unroll, salt again (use table salt). Stretch inside out and dry in the shade.

If possible, with no delays in shipping, cut, as above, leaving skin on the head and salt heavily. Ship at once!

# BIG GAME SKINNING ON THE GROUND

ONE MAN SKINNING A SPIKE BULL ELK.

Chapter 3

Big Game

REMOVE THE INNARDS AS USUAL IF MEAT IS TO BE SAVED. SLIT THE SKIN FROM BELLY TO THROAT (UNLESS THE HEAD IS TO BE MOUNTED). NOW SLIT THE LEGS' SKIN, INSIDE, FROM THE BELLY SLIT TO AND AROUND THE HOOF OR PADS (LEAVE 2 JOINTS AND A CLAW OF EACH TOE ATTACHED TO BEAR SKINS, ETCETERA). SKIN THE LEGS AND BODY OF ONE SIDE AS FAR AROUND THE BACK AS YOU CAN GO WITH THE BEAST ON ITS SIDE. STRETCH THIS SKIN ON THE GROUND AND ROLL THE SKINNED CARCASS OVER ON IT. NOW SKIN OUT THE OTHER EXPOSED SIDE TO COMPLETE THE JOB.

Chapter 3
Big Game

# LARGE SKINS ARE CLUMSY TO CARRY

**B**EAR OR OTHER LARGE TROPHY SKINS OR CAPE WITH HEAD ATTACHED, CAN BE CARRIED ON A PACKBOARD.

**I**N SKINNING OUT A BEAR, SEPARATE THE SKIN FROM THE FAT, LEAVING THE FAT ON THE CARCASS. LATER ON IT IS MORE DIFFICULT TO REMOVE FAT, AND THE PELT MAY WEIGH OVER 25 LBS. WITHOUT IT.

**T**HE PELT SHOULD BE FREE OF ALL BLOOD OR EXCRETA. NEXT, IT MAY BE TIED INTO A TIGHT ROLL WITH A ROPE AT THE MIDDLE AND ENDS. LACKING A PACKBOARD, THE "HORSESHOE" CARRY IS IDEAL. UNROLL AT CAMP.

# MIGHTY MITE

A LIGHT WEIGHT BLOCK AND TACKLE THAT WEIGHS ONLY 17 OZ. BUT LIFTS UP TO 1,000 LBS. IS A HANDY THING FOR HOISTING.

Pocket-size, it's most useful in moving sheep, deer, etc. out of difficult spots, off ledges, out of steep canyons, etc. If one hunts alone it may be necessary to hang a dressed carcass off the ground while he goes for helpers to pack the game out. With this, he won't need muscle to hang it!

**Chapter 3**

**Big Game**

**Chapter 3**
**Big Game**

# ONE MAN JOB...

Try this if camp is too far to pack your deer without help. Climb a nearby sapling that bends with your weight. Tie your utility rope on the sapling where it bends well after placing deer in position. Hold rope tight against antlers until tied up short to sapling. Release your weight. If need be, use props to lift off ground.

# HANGING BIG GAME BY ONE MAN

**Chapter 3**

**Big Game**

FIELD DRESS THE GAME FIRST TO REDUCE THE WEIGHT. CUT A GAMBREL SLIT IN EACH HIND LEG. FIND A STRAIGHT POLE AT LEAST 20 FT. LONG, STRONG ENOUGH TO SUPPORT THE CARCASS AND LEAN ONE END IN A TREE FORK. WITH THE BEAST ON ITS BACK, INSERT A GAMBREL STICK THROUGH THE HIND LEG SLITS, PINNING THE LEGS AROUND THE POLE. SLIDE HANGING GAME UP THE LEANING POLE UNTIL IT'S OFF THE GROUND. TIE GAMBREL STICK TO THE POLE.

Chapter 3

Big Game

# LEAVING YOUR TROPHY GUARDED IN THE FIELD......

HANDKERCHIEF

Do NOT ALLOW GAME TO LIE ON THE GROUND ANY LONGER THAN IS NECESSARY AFTER DRESSING IT OUT, ELSE IT SPOILS QUICKLY!

If IT IS TOO HEAVY TO MOVE BY YOURSELF, WORK TREE LIMBS, STICKS, ROCKS, ETC. UNDER THE PRIZE TO RAISE IT OFF THE GROUND.

Cover IT WITH PINE, SPRUCE OR FIR TYPE BOUGHS IF POSSIBLE (AS ABOVE) TO SHED RAIN OR SNOW. USE ROCKS TO WEIGHT DOWN IF WIND IS LIKELY. THIS COVERING OR OTHER BRUSH KEEPS PREDATORY BIRDS AWAY. A HANDKERCHIEF KEEPS COYOTES AWAY BUT NOT OTHER <u>ANIMAL</u> PREDATORS.

# HOW TO RELOCATE CACHED GAME....

Chapter 3

Big Game

It is usually easier to find your way back to camp or out of the woods than it is to return to an exact spot. Often a single hunter must leave a heavy trophy to get help to pack it out. In his excitement over his success, he may forget to orient himself to his surroundings so that he can easily return. Thus, he may lose his prize!

Heavy woods and swamps without a trail or landmarks are the most difficult. For such areas, use a small axe or knife to mark trees on the way out. Rock piles or sticks may be used also.

# A ONE MAN CARRY FOR BIG GAME....

Chapter 3
Big Game

TIE A RED HANDKER-CHIEF ON THE ANTLERS

SLIT FRONT LEGS' SKIN FROM JUST ABOVE KNEE TO HALF-WAY TO FOOT. PEEL SKIN BACK SO YOU CAN SEVER THE KNEE JOINT. CUT A 2" SLIT IN THE REAR LEGS' GAMBREL THROUGH WHICH THE FRONT LEG IS PASSED TO LOCK AS SHOWN. SLIP ARMS INTO PACK-SACK-LIKE CARRY BY LYING DOWN.

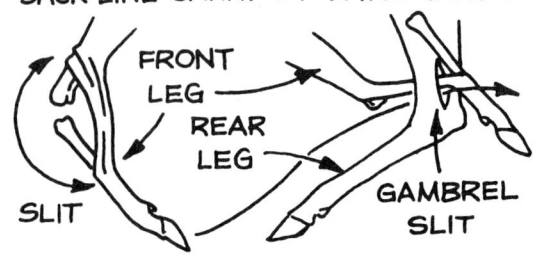

FRONT LEG
REAR LEG
SLIT
GAMBREL SLIT

**Chapter 3**

**Big Game**

EASY TWO-MAN CARRIER IS MADE BY PLACING TWO TEN FOOT POLES, THREE INCHES IN DIAMETER, TWENTY INCHES APART ALONGSIDE OF DEER. TIE ONE END OF 3/8 INCH ROPE 50 FOOT LONG, EVEN WITH TAIL AND LACE FORWARD TO HEAD. TIE EACH ANTLER TO A POLE, AFTER ROLLING DEER ONTO STRETCHER.

WALK OUT-OF-STEP WITH PARTNER TO ACHIEVE A BETTER BALANCE.

# HAULING BIG GAME

Chapter 3

Big Game

Here's a neat way to haul a deer or other big game in to camp without too much trouble.

It's a heavy weight piece of canvas about 4 ft. wide and 9 ft. long. Place grommets 6 in. apart at one end, 1 inch from the edge, to lace it to a cut pole with light rope when in use. Tie game's antlers or head to pole and sled it out!

No chance of marring a skin!

# IT'S HANDSOME TO SEE BUT IT RUINS THE BEST FLAVOR!

Chapter 3

Big Game

Envious admiring glances of fellow hunters, friends and the wife, are not hard for the deerslayer to take. It's a grand feeling, I know, but it ruins the BEST flavor to expose prized game to the sun or motor heat by dressing your car front as above.

The carcass should be cooled as quickly as possible in the shade. For returning home, wrap it in canvas and fasten on the car's top, or in states permitting, quarter and place in car's trunk, but do not tie on near the motor!

# TRAPPING

Trapping is a soul-satisfying hobby which has close ties with the adventurous, romantic past. It pits the cunning of a man or boy against that of small mammals and beasts, from muskrat to mountain lion. It is a fine midwinter outdoor sport, and trappers provide a service to the community by keeping predatory animals under control. Since professional trapping has decreased in volume, fur animals have been increasing — foxes may now be found where 20 years ago there were practically none.

Here and there, the trapper may find a trophy for his game room or den. Tanning and mounting a trophy is a job for a taxidermist.

As a profession, trapping provides comparatively small pay. This wasn't so in the early days of the United States. But, in recent years, prices of pelts have gone down and the market for furs has been unstable. Moreover, trappers are faced with high shipping charges to get their furs to market, and are almost forced to take the first offer, whether it's fair or not! The result is that most of the professionals have left the field to school-age boys who tend their trap-lines before and after school.

The most reliable market for a young trapper is a local furrier who processes his own garments. Second best are the well-known mail-order houses, who buy furs, and sell through catalogs. The individual trapper today has the fur farms to compete with, and these produce furs by the thousand in size, color and texture as the market demands.

In all fur houses, price depends upon the grade and condition of the fur. Cold climate furs bring higher prices than those from warmer climates, but the southern trapper may make just as much money because he can trap more easily without worrying about adverse weather conditions.

# MUSKRAT TRAPPING

**Chapter 4 — Trapping**

A CHOICE LOCATION FOR A MUSKRAT TRAP IS IN WATER FROM 1 TO 3 IN. DEEP UNDER AN OVERHANGING BANK. A ROCK OR LOG MAY BE PLACED TO DIRECT A...

...SWIMMING MUSKRAT TO PASS BETWEEN IT AND THE BANK. A MUSKRAT PREFERS TO STAY NEAR THE BANK WHEN HE TRAVELS AGAINST THE CURRENT, SO POINT THE TRAP SPRING UPSTREAM. THEN ITS RELEASE CAN'T KNOCK A FOOT ASIDE.

USE A NO. 1½ TRAP. IT TAKES A HIGHER HOLD THAN A NO. 1 AND IT WILL TAKE MINK AND COON THAT USE THE SAME ROUTE. LET SUCH TRAPS RUST TO PREVENT DETECTION AND <u>THEFT</u>!

# TRAP MUSKRATS ON A FLOATING PLANK

TRAPS PARTLY HIDDEN BY GRASS

BAIT

Chapter 4

Trapping

Select a wide board that won't tip over easily in water. Nail several traps to the board. Place sardines, fish, cut chunks of turtle or apples between traps so rats will step in traps getting at bait. Nail bait onto board. Scatter straw or grass over traps. Anchor the board in a slough or backwater where current is slow moving or absent.

Often more than one rat is caught at the same time!

# ANCHORING THE MUSKRAT TRAP.....

**E**XTRA CHAIN OR WIRE MAY....

Chapter 4

Trapping

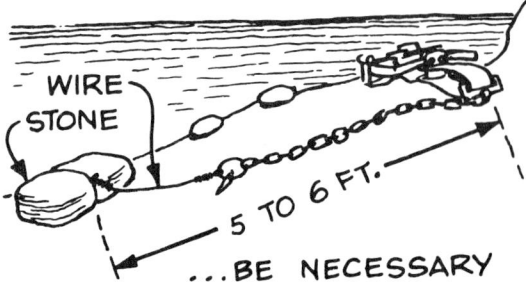

...BE NECESSARY TO LENGTHEN THE TRAP CHAIN TO 5 OR 6 FT. A SHORTER CHAIN WOULD PERMIT A MUSKRAT TO SWIM OUT IN THE STREAM AS FAR AS HE COULD AND <u>RETURN</u> TO SHALLOW WATER WITHOUT TIRING ENOUGH TO DROWN BUT A LONG CHAIN CAUSES HIS FAILURE.

**P**ICK A FLAT STONE ABOUT 12 IN. LONG, 4 IN. WIDE AND 1 OR 2 IN. THICK. CUT NOTCHES AROUND ITS MIDDLE TO KEEP THE WIRE FROM SLIPPING OFF. AFTER THE TRAP IS SET NEAR SHORE, TOSS THE STONE OUT IN THE STREAM BUT BE SURE THE CHAIN LIES ON THE STREAM'S BOTTOM SO THAT FLOATING DEBRIS CAN'T ENTANGLE IT AND MOVE TRAP.

# USING A STAKE FOR TRAPPED MUSKRATS

Place a stick out in the deeper water (at least...

Chapter 4

Trapping

...10 inches deep) about three feet beyond the flat stone anchor. Push stick 6 inches into the mud.

When caught, the muskrat usually swims out to the stick, circling it until the wrapped chain drowns him.

Chapter 4

Trapping

# ANIMAL LURE TIPS FOR TRAPPING.....

Use only one brand of lure at each set. They may have a similar odor but they are different. Don't use a coon lure for fox, etc. If you want to try several different fox lures to find the best for YOUR area, don't place sets closer than 100 ft. apart in a field

Use lure sparingly. 1 or 2 drops is usual at a new set. Add 1 drop after rain. A medicine dropper is handy to use.

Lure is most valued for fox, coon, weasel and coyote.

Use strong 'WINTER-TYPE' lure in below freezing weather!

# COON TRAPPING...

*PLACE TRAP IN 5 OR 6 INCHES OF WATER*

**Chapter 4**

Trapping

A COON LIKES TO FOLLOW THE EDGE OF A STREAM IN SEARCH OF FOOD. IN CLEAR WATER HIS TRACKS MAY BE SEEN EIGHT INCHES DEEP AS HE IS FORCED TO WADE TO AVOID AN OBSTRUCTION IN HIS PATH ALONG THE BANK. THIS IS THE BEST PLACE TO PLACE YOUR TRAP.

THIS "SET" WILL NOT TAKE MUSKRATS AS THEY SWIM, NOT WADE, AT THIS DEPTH.

Chapter 4
Trapping

# A STUMP SET FOR TRAPPING COON

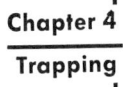

COVERED TRAP

PARTLY COVERED BAIT (FISH, SARDINE, FRUIT, ETC.)

ONE OR TWO DROPS OF COON LURE

Select an old stump about 2 or 3 ft. high having a rotten top. Dig a bed in the top to fit the set trap, then cover with tissue paper or leaves and sprinkle bits of the rotten wood over it. Place bait beside the trap and use some coon lure nearby. Fix trap-chain to a tree-limb drag. Smelling lure, coon climbs stump to investigate and is caught.

# THE BEAVER LODGE

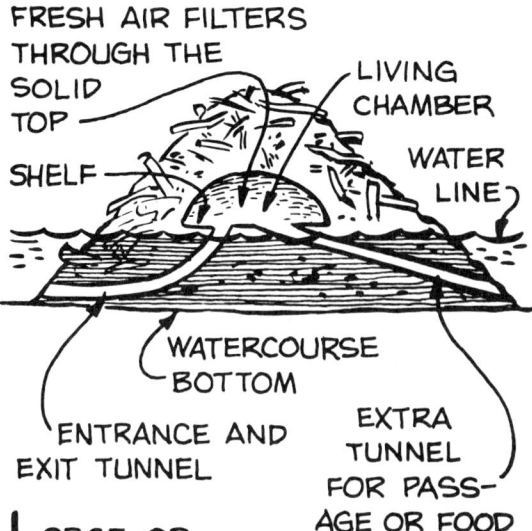

FRESH AIR FILTERS THROUGH THE SOLID TOP

LIVING CHAMBER

SHELF

WATER LINE

WATERCOURSE BOTTOM

ENTRANCE AND EXIT TUNNEL

EXTRA TUNNEL FOR PASSAGE OR FOOD SUPPLY

Chapter 4

Trapping

LODGE OR HOUSE IS BEGUN WITH THE BEAVERS PILING UP A FOUNDATION OF STONES, MUD, STICKS, TWIGS, SMALL TREES AND LOGS INTO A TIGHT LACED SOLID MASS. DOME SHAPED, THIS MOUND RISES SEVERAL FEET ABOVE THE WATER AND MAY BE 20 FEET IN DIAMETER.

TUNNELS ARE CUT UNDERWATER NEAR THE BOTTOM AS SHOWN ABOVE. THE LIVING ROOM IS CUT OUT IN THE CENTER, ABOVE THE WATER. FINISHED, IT'S A DRY, SNUG AND SAFE HOME.

Chapter 4

Trapping

# WEASEL TRAPPING

WEASELS FEED UPON RABBITS, SQUIRRELS, CHIPMUNKS, GAME BIRDS, POULTRY, ETC. RUTHLESS KILLERS, OFTEN KILLING MORE THAN THEY CAN EAT, THEY WILL NEVERTHELESS BE ATTRACTED TO FRESH KILLED MEAT. NAIL A RABBIT HEAD TO A TREE ONE FOOT ABOVE THE GROUND. SET THE TRAP BELOW AND COVER IT WITH GRASS, LEAVES OR WITH SNOW--FIRST COVER THE PAN WITH A PIECE OF PAPER OR WHITE CLOTH.

# TRAP WEASELS IN THIS "LOG SET"....

*(Illustration: weasel on a dry, hollow log (off ground) with TRAP, SPRING, BAIT labeled, points A and B marked)*

**Chapter 4**

**Trapping**

Save small game by trapping this predator for his fur and a bounty in some states.

Use ½ of an easily caught mouse for bait. Dip it in glycerin to prevent its freezing in cold weather. Frozen bait gives off no scent. Pour a few drops of weasel lure (A) under the bait, <u>NOT ON IT</u>, about 12 inches back in hollow log. Set the trap (a no. 0, 1, or 1½) with spring toward bait so it won't knock weasel aside in releasing. Fix trap chain to a drag or sapling. Pour a few drops of lure on outside of log (B). Grease waxed traps with lard (not oil) to ease action.

Chapter 4
Trapping

## USING A "BOX SET" TO TRAP WEASELS

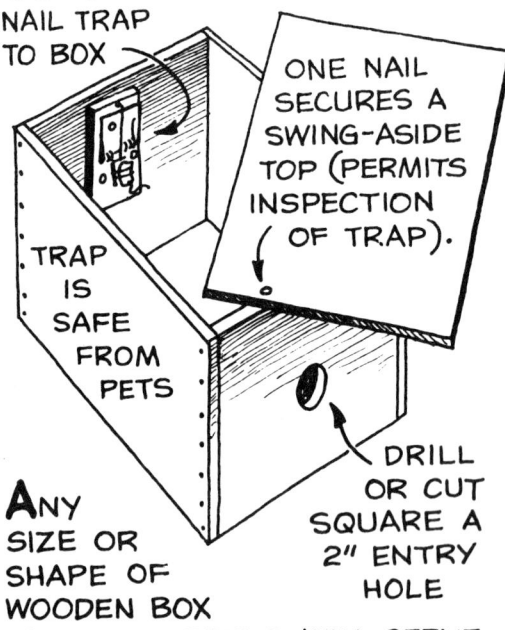

NAIL TRAP TO BOX

ONE NAIL SECURES A SWING-ASIDE TOP (PERMITS INSPECTION OF TRAP).

TRAP IS SAFE FROM PETS

DRILL OR CUT SQUARE A 2" ENTRY HOLE

Any size or shape of wooden box will do. Ground will serve for the bottom. A rock may be added to hold the top down. Nail an ordinary barn rat trap onto an inside wall so its trigger points down when set, about 7 or 8 inches above ground. Use fine wire to tie ½ of a mouse to the trigger for bait. Pour a few drops of weasel lure on the trap (NOT BAIT) and box top.

# THE TRAPPER'S CUBBY PEN SET....

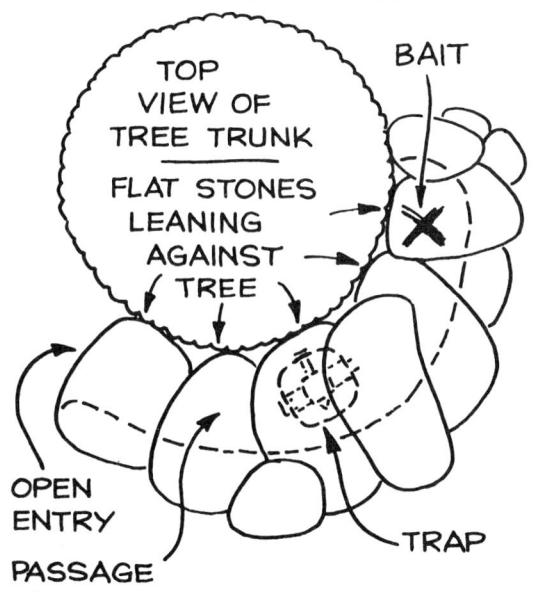

Chapter 4

Trapping

TOP VIEW OF TREE TRUNK

FLAT STONES LEANING AGAINST TREE

BAIT

OPEN ENTRY PASSAGE

TRAP

All fur bearers are more or less curious and spend a great deal of time exploring their domain. Here is a good set for weasel, skunk, opossum, etcetera. Lean the stones to form a passage, closed at one end. The trap should be concealed by leaves and the bait placed before passage is covered.

Place scent drops in passage.

Chapter 4 — Trapping

# HOW TO LOCATE FOXES BY "SIGNS"

WALK AN OLD DIRT COUNTRY ROAD AND LOOK FOR TRACKS IN SOFT SPOTS OR DROPPINGS ON THE HIGH HUMPS OR ROCKS. IT IS A CHARACTERISTIC OF THE FOX TO SELECT SUCH PLACES IN A ROAD IT TRAVELS. IF THE DROPPINGS CONTAIN APPLE SEEDS, THE FOX HAS BEEN FEEDING NEARBY IN AN ORCHARD. PARTS OF CRICKETS, GRASSHOPPERS, ETC., INDICATE A FIELD OR MEADOW. FOXES PREFER OPEN FIELDS TO HEAVY BRUSH FOR DEPREDATION.

# FOX TRAPPING TIP

Chapter 4

Trapping

SELECT A KNOLL OR SMALL HILL FACING TOWARD A TREE ABOUT 20 FEET AWAY. HANG A SMALL CHICKEN IN THE TREE SOME 10 FEET ABOVE THE GROUND. SCOOP OUT DIRT OR SNOW ON THE HILL TO DRIVE A CHAIN-STAKE, FOLD CHAIN AND SET TRAP OVER IT. COVER AND LEVEL THE SET AND YOUR TRACKS WITH A TREE BRANCH AS YOU BACKTRACK BEYOND THE TREE TO YOUR TRAIL. FRUSTRATED FOX GOES TO THE KNOLL TO SIT, HOWL AND BE <u>TRAPPED</u>!

Chapter 4
Trapping

# DIRT HOLE FOX 'SET'

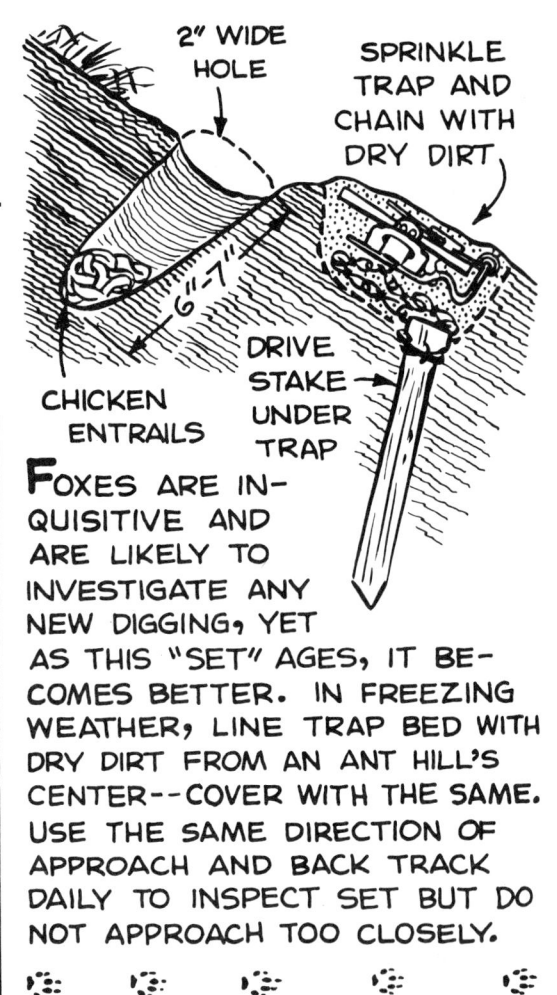

2" WIDE HOLE

SPRINKLE TRAP AND CHAIN WITH DRY DIRT

6"-7"

CHICKEN ENTRAILS

DRIVE STAKE UNDER TRAP

Foxes are inquisitive and are likely to investigate any new digging, yet as this "SET" ages, it becomes better. In freezing weather, line trap bed with dry dirt from an ant hill's center--cover with the same. Use the same direction of approach and back track daily to inspect set but do not approach too closely.

FOX TRACKS ARE NEAT AND IN A STRAIGHT LINE.

# WHERE FOX TRAPPING IS PERMITTED.......

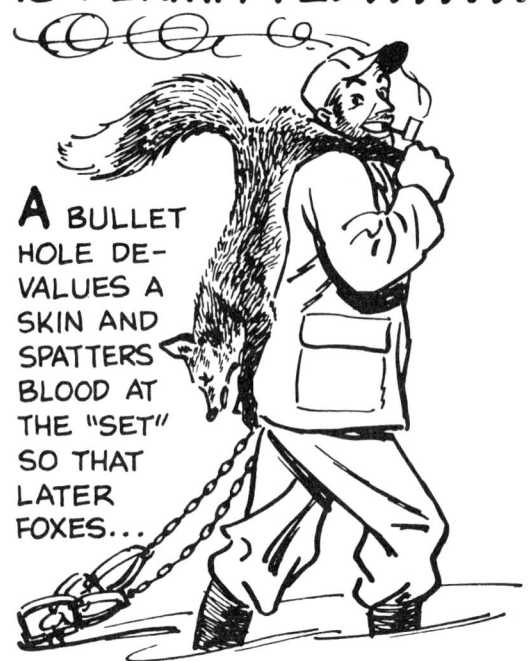

Chapter 4

Trapping

A BULLET HOLE DE-VALUES A SKIN AND SPATTERS BLOOD AT THE "SET" SO THAT LATER FOXES...

...WILL AVOID IT, THUS A NEW TRAP LOCATION MUST BE FOUND. THE MOST PAINLESS WAY TO A-VOID THIS AND INSURE FURTHER CATCHES IS THE USE OF A FORK-ED STICK TO HOLD A FOX DOWN AND THEN STEPPING ON ITS BODY IN BACK OF AND UNDER ITS RIGHT FORE LEG OVER THE HEART. PRESENTLY, HEART BEAT STOPS. A MORE VALUED PELT RESULTS.

**Chapter 4**

**Trapping**

# DE-ODOR, COLOR AND WAX TRAPS FOR BETTER TRAPPING RESULTS!

Boil new or used traps in a clean lard can or wash boiler filled with a solution of water and Red Seal Lye for an hour. Use separate wires from underwater chains to support. Hook above to remove traps. This boiling removes all odors from traps.

Remove traps separately and dump water. Rinse, refill with water only, then add several walnut hulls, maple leaves (or bark) or buy log-wood crystals. A nail holds the trap jaws open. For all-over color of blue or brown, boil several hours. Reduce to a simmer. Cut beeswax in to cover surface, then slowly remove each trap.

# LEAD FUR BEARERS TO YOUR TRAPS....

Chapter 4

Trapping

IN SOME LOCALITIES FUR BEARERS ARE SCATTERED AND IT WILL PAY TO OPEN THE CARCASS OF A SKINNED ANIMAL AND DRAG IT BEHIND YOU AS YOU MAKE YOUR ROUNDS ON THE TRAPLINE. SCENT IT HEAVILY TO ADD TO ITS APPEAL.

FUR BEARERS CROSSING YOUR TRAIL ARE INCLINED TO FOLLOW THIS DRAG TO YOUR TRAPS.

# TRAPPING TRICKS: THE TRAP DRAG

LEAVE THE BRANCHES ON

ATTACH IN THE CENTER

1½" TO 2" THICK

**S**KUNKS, OPPOSSUM, COON AND VARIOUS OTHER FUR BEARERS WILL NOT STRUGGLE SO HARD TO ESCAPE IF THE TRAP CHAIN IS WIRED TO A TREE LIMB OR SAPLING 5 OR 6 FT. LONG. WHEN IT'S NOT FIXED SOLID, THEY CAN MOVE IT AND THINK THEY'RE ESCAPING.

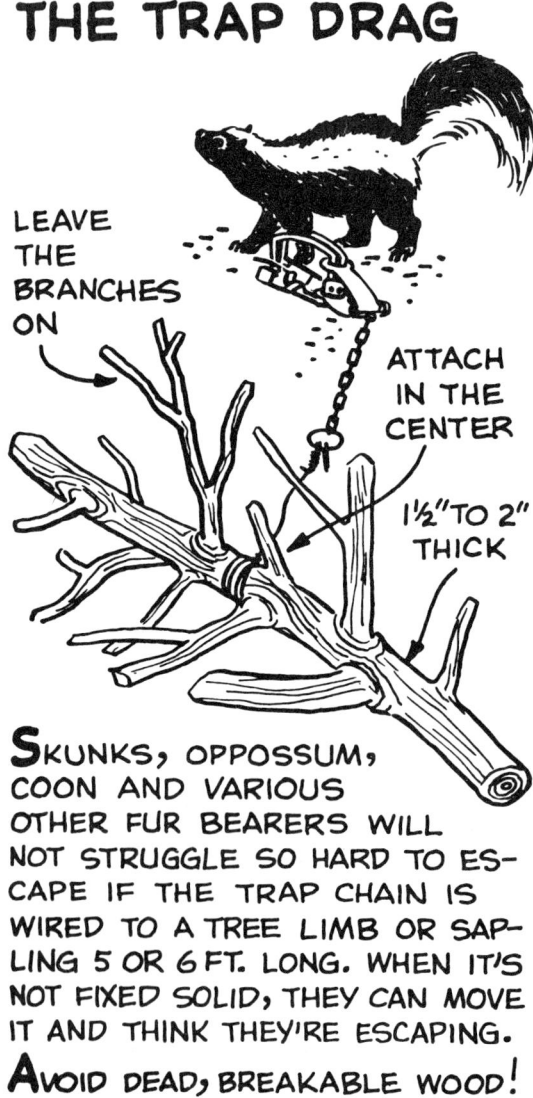

**A**VOID DEAD, BREAKABLE WOOD!

# EASY SQUIRREL SKINNING METHOD

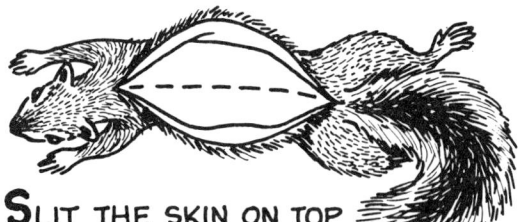

Chapter 4

Trapping

SLIT THE SKIN ON TOP OF THE BACK FROM THE TAIL TO THE SHOULDERS. WORK THE SKIN LOOSE WITH YOUR FINGERS (AND KNIFE IF NECESSARY). PUSH THE SKIN DOWN AND AWAY FROM THE BODY WITH YOUR THUMBS. AFTER LOOSENING THE SKIN <u>ALL THE WAY AROUND THE BODY</u> HOLD THE SKIN UNDER THE BELLY IN ONE HAND AND GRASP THE BODY AROUND THE MIDDLE WITH THE OTHER HAND. NOW PULL. THE SKIN COMES OFF INSIDE OUT.

SKIN

PULL EACH LEG OUT SEPARATELY WITH YOUR FINGERS. CUT OFF THE FEET, TAIL AND HEAD. SOME COOKS LIKE TO USE THE HEAD. IF SO, DON'T CUT IT OFF. PULL IT OUT OF THE SKIN, CUT FREE THE EARS, EYES AND NOSE.

Chapter 4

Trapping

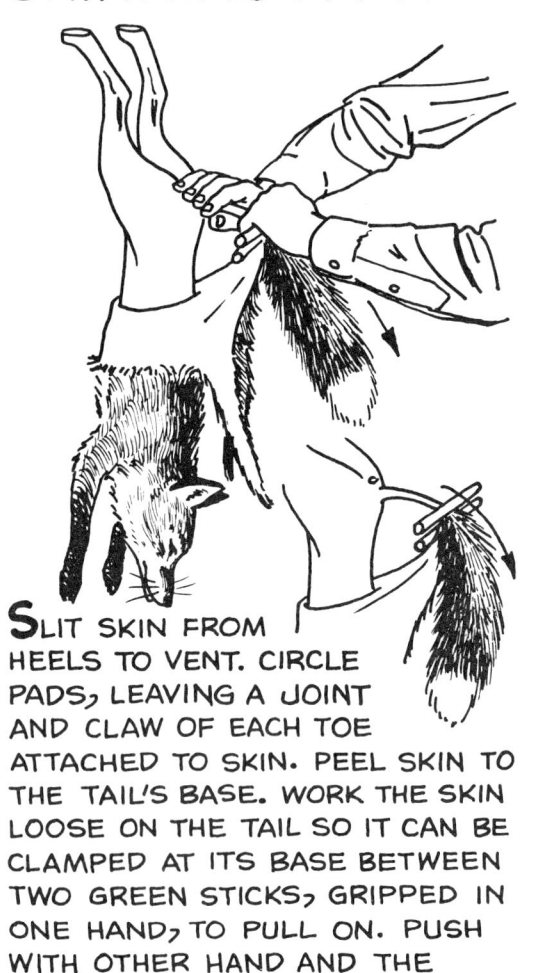

# SKINNING A FOX...

Slit skin from heels to vent. Circle pads, leaving a joint and claw of each toe attached to skin. Peel skin to the tail's base. Work the skin loose on the tail so it can be clamped at its base between two green sticks, gripped in one hand, to pull on. Push with other hand and the brush slips off the tail. Peel body skin on down. Leave toes, ears, nose and lips on skin.

# FUR SKINNING TIPS

Hang animal by its hind legs on cords with a lariat knot for each foot. Remove one foot at a time to skin legs.

Chapter 4

Trapping

Skinning is easiest as soon as possible after catching. Hang by hind legs if forced to delay until next day. If wet, shake to loosen thick underfur to aid drying. Dry all furs and comb clean dried mud, burs, etc., before skinning.

To case-skin: slit from heels to and around vent. Cut off foot pads. Leave last toe joints and claws on skin. Pull out tail bone. Peel skin, inside out. Free front toes, ears at base, etc. with knife.

Chapter 4
Trapping

# HOW TO TAN A PELT
# – PRELIMINARIES –

**R**UB SALT ON A RAW GREEN SKIN'S FLESH SIDE TO "CURE" IT. DRY FLESH SIDE OUT

**A**FTER SKIN IS COMPLETELY DRIED IN A COOL AIRY SPOT (NO SUN), IT IS THEN READY TO SOFTEN FOR THE "FLESHING" (REMOVING ALL REMAINING TRACES OF FAT, FLESH, MEMBRANES AND GRISTLE.)

1 LB. SALT    2 GAL. WATER

**M**IX A SOLUTION IN A LARGE TUB TO COVER SKIN CONSISTING OF 1 LB. OF SALT TO EVERY 2 GALLONS OF WATER USED. SOAK COMPLETELY COVERED SKIN 8 HOURS. REMOVE SKIN AND HANG TO DRAIN THEN RUB EXTRA SALT IN FLESH SIDE. FOLD SKIN ONCE, FLESH SIDE IN, ROLL, LEAVE OVERNIGHT.

**T**HIS LOOSENS REMAINING FLESH.

# TANNING SMALL SKINS............

**M**IX ONE QUART OF TABLE SALT IN ONE GALLON OF <u>SOFT</u> WATER. HEAT UNTIL THE SALT IS DISSOLVED. THEN LET IT COOL IN AN EARTHENWARE CROCK OR A WOODEN BUCKET BEFORE STIRRING IN ONE OUNCE OF SULPHURIC ACID.

**R**EMOVE FAT AND FLESH FROM SKINS FIRST. USE SALT TO DRY STRETCHED SKINS. THEN, SOAK SQUIRREL, MUSKRAT OR OTHER SKIN IN SOLUTION ABOVE FOR 5 DAYS, STIRRED DAILY. REMOVE AND RINSE IN CLEAR WATER. SOAK 12 HRS. IN MIX OF 1 GAL. WATER TO ½ CUP SAL SODA. RINSE AGAIN. RUB SKIN SIDES TOGETHER AND KEEP MOIST UNTIL IT DRIES SOFT.

Chapter 4

Trapping

Chapter 4
Trapping

# HOW TO TAN A PELT

Dissolve 2 lbs. of alum in boiling water. Mix 5 lbs. of salt in 10 gallons of water and add the dissolved alum. Stir until mixed. If more solution is needed, mix in proportion to cover pelt.

Soak small game skins 3 days, coon to wolf sizes 5 days and bear sizes 10 days. During this time slosh the skin up and down and stir it three times daily.

Remove skin and rinse in running water or submerge it skin side up but weighted with rocks in a stream until no salt taste remains (test by tongue). Stretch skin to partly dry in shade. Before it has dried completely, remove and begin "breaking" to soften it by daily pulling it over the rounded end of a plank driven into the ground. Keep it moist. Finish flesh side with tanning oil.

# HOW TO TAN A PELT
## "FLESHING"

**A** SIMPLE FLESHING BEAM IS A WIDE PLANK, ROUND OFF THE PLANK'S TOP AND EDGE WITH A PLANE. SUPPORTED AT ONE END BY A SAW-HORSE AND RESTING THE OTHER END ON THE GROUND. A SMOOTHED ROUND TREE TRUNK, SPLIT IN HALF WITH THE BARK REMOVED, MAKES A GOOD FLESHING BEAM ALSO.

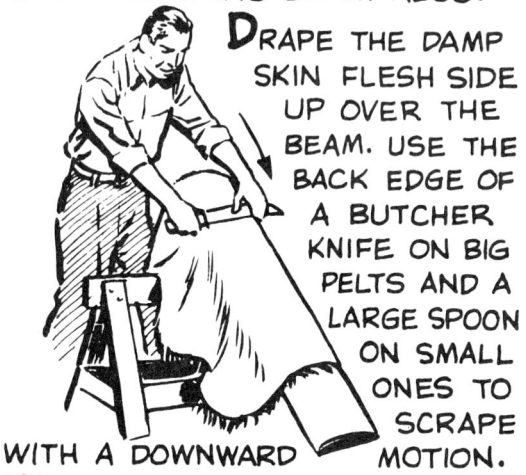

Chapter 4
Trapping

**D**RAPE THE DAMP SKIN FLESH SIDE UP OVER THE BEAM. USE THE BACK EDGE OF A BUTCHER KNIFE ON BIG PELTS AND A LARGE SPOON ON SMALL ONES TO SCRAPE WITH A DOWNWARD MOTION.

**W**HEN ALL FLESH IS REMOVED, HANG PELT IN <u>SHADE</u> TO DRY.

# A SKIN STRETCHER FOR BIG GAME USE IS EASY TO MAKE

**Chapter 4**

**Trapping**

REMOVE ALL FAT OR FLESH, SALT THE INSIDE HEAVILY, PEPPER THE HAIR SIDE. SALT DAILY. DRIES IN A WEEK.

**B**EAR, MOUNTAIN LION, MOOSE OR ANY LARGE TROPHY SKINS MAY BE STRETCHED THIS WAY IN A PERMANENT CAMP. LASH TOGETHER 4 POLES OF 3 IN. DIAMETER TO FORM A FRAME LARGER THAN THE SKIN. CUT CORD HOLES 6 IN. APART, ½ IN. FROM THE SKIN'S EDGE AND STRETCH WITH HEAVY CORD.

# BETTER MARKSMANSHIP

Select a gun powerful enough for the game you seek, then learn to shoot it accurately! Some sportsmen never shoot their guns between regular seasons, except for a few rounds before the season opens. If half of their shots strike anywhere on the target, some fellows feel they are ready for the real thing. I saw one chap, for example, who couldn't hit the target from fifty yards. It didn't bother him because he was using a borrowed gun and would use a different one for the hunt.

One should always "sight-in" a gun which will be used, by careful target shooting. Thus one knows exactly where to hold for the correct range. The gun should be as familiar to you as your arms and legs. From there on it's knowing how to hunt. Learn all you can about the habits of game and get as close as possible for the first shot. Make it a good one because it usually is your best opportunity.

# EDUCATE TO AVOID GUN ACCIDENTS!

Chapter 5

Better Marksmanship

A LARGE PERCENTAGE OF ALL GUN CASUALTIES ARE NOT CAUSED IN ACTUAL HUNTING! IGNORANCE AND CARELESSNESS CAUSE MANY OF THESE IN THE HOME ITSELF!

THE NATIONAL RIFLE ASSOCIATION'S COLLECTED STATISTICS SHOW THAT, IN <u>ACTUAL</u> HUNTING, MORE THAN <u>ONE-THIRD</u> OF ALL CASUALTIES ARE CAUSED BY PERSONS <u>19</u> YEARS OR LESS IN AGE! BUT AMONG THE YOUTH GROUPS INSTRUCTED BY N.R.A., RIFLE CLUBS OR SOME PUBLIC SCHOOLS THERE WERE PRACTICALLY <u>NO</u> ACCIDENTS IN HUNTING! QUALIFIED INSTRUCTION PREVENTS NEEDLESS ACCIDENTS!

# SAFE GUN RULES

Never take a handed gun or pick one up by the muzzle!

Chapter 5

Better Marksmanship

① HANDLE <u>ANY</u> GUN AS IF IT WERE LOADED!
② UNLOAD GUN AND OPEN ITS ACTION BEFORE ENTERING AN AUTOMOBILE, HOME OR CAMP!
③ ALWAYS BE SURE BARREL AND ACTION ARE OBSTRUCTION-CLEAR!
④ CARRY GUN SO MUZZLE DIRECTION IS ALWAYS CONTROLLED, EVEN IN A STUMBLE!
⑤ DON'T FIRE AT <u>UNKNOWN</u> TARGETS!
⑥ NEVER POINT GUN AT ANYTHING YOU DON'T WANT TO KILL!
⑦ UNLOAD UNGUARDED GUNS!
⑧ NEVER CLIMB TREES OR FENCES WITH A LOADED GUN!
⑨ NEVER SHOOT AT FLAT, HARD SURFACES OR WATER SURFACES!
⑩ DON'T MIX ALCOHOL & HUNTING!

**Chapter 5**

Better Marksmanship

# IT'S WISE TO WEAR SHOOTING GLASSES

TINTED SHOOTING GLASSES ARE A GREAT HELP WHEN SHOOTING INTO THE SUN AT GAME. THE BEST HUNTING HOURS OF THE DAY ARE WHEN THE SUN MAY BE RIGHT IN YOUR EYES.

SHOOTER'S EYES ARE SAFELY PROTECTED FROM AN ACCIDENTAL BACKFIRE OF GAS, UNBURNED POWDER, ETC. IF A PRIMER OR CASE SHOULD BE RUPTURED WHEN FIRING NON-HAMMERLESS TYPES OF GUNS!

# SMART GUN TIP!

**Chapter 5**

Better Marksmanship

When two or more hunters are hunting together, it is a safe practice to keep loads out of their gun chambers until ready to fire. Thus, there is NO danger of an accidental discharge for any reason! When game is sighted, it only takes a split second to chamber a load from the magazine by pump, lever or bolt. If a hunter is by himself or on a "stand", a loaded gun with its safety on is usually safe.

Invariably a hunter has ample time for this precaution.

# HUNT SAFELY AND AVOID ACCIDENTS

Chapter 5

Better Marksmanship

RIGHT-HANDED HUNTERS SHOULD NEVER CARRY THEIR GUNS POINTED IN THE GENERAL DIRECTION OF A BUDDY ON THEIR LEFT, EVEN IF THE SAFETY IS ON! EITHER POINT GUN OVER RIGHT SHOULDER OR STRAIGHT AHEAD. A CENTER-HUNTER ACTS LIKEWISE. LEFT-HANDERS, NEVER TOWARDS MEN ON THEIR RIGHT. SOME "OLD TIMERS", AS WELL AS YOUNG SPORTSMEN, OFTEN VIOLATE THIS RULE!

# AVOIDING ACCIDENTS

Chapter 5

Better Marksmanship

These hunters are risking a tragic accident.

Never point a gun muzzle carelessly at a friend or at <u>anything</u> you wouldn't shoot! Many sportsmen frequently break this rule.

Don't climb fences with a loaded gun. Instead, set it down where its trigger can not be accidently snagged while climbing over. Hunting pals should hand the guns over for safety.

# OFFHAND SHOTS

**Chapter 5**

Better Marksmanship

EVERY HUNTER SHOULD STRIVE TOWARD BECOMING AN EXPERT OFFHAND MARKSMAN! REGARDLESS OF WHERE HE HUNTS IT IS OFTEN THE ONLY SHOOTING POSITION HE IS OFFERED BECAUSE OF TERRAIN, BRUSH, HIGH GRASS, ETC. WHICH WOULD OBSCURE THE TARGET IF HE WERE PRONE OR EVEN KNEELING. THE 'WHITE HUNTER' GUIDES OF AFRICA USE THIS POSITION WHEN FACED BY DANGEROUS GAME TO PROTECT A CLIENT OR THEIR OWN LIVES.

# BREATHE DEEPLY BEFORE SHOOTING

**Chapter 5**

Better Marksmanship

Exertion from a difficult stalk or climb to get within range of game for a shot or the exciting anticipation of a shot makes it difficult to keep the gunsight on the target, lessening your chances for a good shot.

Take a few deep breaths and exhale about two thirds of the last one, holding the rest within. Now, aim! You've forced enough oxygen into your system to steady you down, lasting for the shot.

If the game hasn't detected your stalk, take time to compose your nerves before shooting. Deep breathing will improve target scores, also!

# SHOOT WITH BOTH EYES OPEN.......

**Chapter 5**

Better Marksmanship

Everyone has a "master eye" that dominates the other eye. It's usually the right eye with right-handed people and left eye with left-handers. Yet it's natural to see BEST with both eyes at once.

Beginners normally squint one eye closed in sighting down a gun-barrel, handicapping themselves with the strain and reducing FULL vision.

Prove it to yourself thus: point your finger at an object across the room with both eyes open. Then close one eye at a time. The "master eye" retains the alignment but the finger jumps away as the other eye is used alone.

With practice you'll sight faster and best with both eyes!

# A BIG ADVANTAGE OF A RIFLE SCOPE SIGHT

A PERFECT SHOT

Chapter 5

Better Marksmanship

Placing the eye in line with the exact center of the scope is <u>unnecessary</u>, whereas when iron sights are used, exact centering <u>is necessary</u>. With a scope, just put the cross hairs (or other reticule) on the mark and squeeze the trigger. The eye may be 1/8 in. off the center yet it's lined up!

The broken center lines used above are only to show eyepiece's exact center. The cross hair is the aim device.

Chapter 5

Better Marksmanship

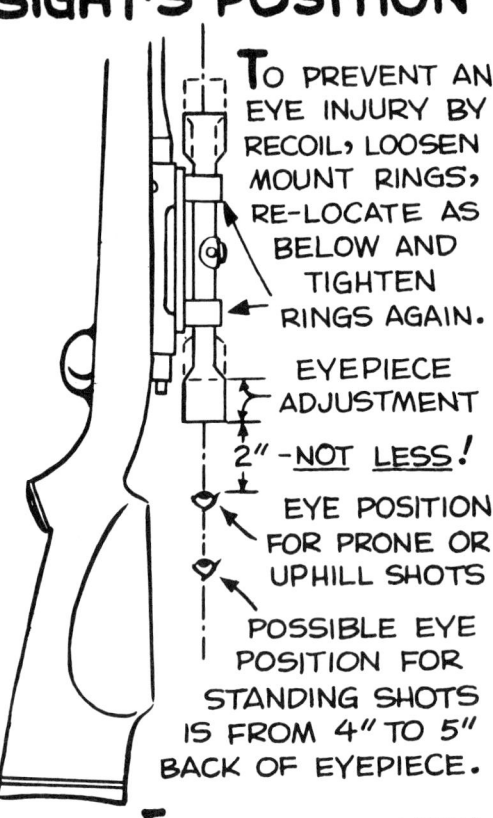

# LOCATING A SCOPE SIGHT'S POSITION

To prevent an eye injury by recoil, loosen mount rings, re-locate as below and tighten rings again.

EYEPIECE ADJUSTMENT

2" - NOT LESS!

EYE POSITION FOR PRONE OR UPHILL SHOTS

POSSIBLE EYE POSITION FOR STANDING SHOTS IS FROM 4" TO 5" BACK OF EYEPIECE.

Full field of view should be seen when ANY shooting position is used. Eyepiece location should not endanger the eye from the gun's recoil. (Suggested from "The American Rifleman")

# TELESCOPE SIGHT FOG PREVENTION

**D**on't carry a telescopic sighted gun between your arm and body on a cold day! It may result in warming the scope above the air temperature so that fog appears to render it useless when a shot is offered!

**D**on't take a cold, scoped gun into your warm camp for the night. Condensation may result and it is likely to fog up when it is taken out into the cold again the next morning. Leave it covered, outside at night, out of reach of camp prowlers!

Chapter 5

Better Marksmanship

# HERE'S A RIFLE SLING CARRY THAT'S FAST TO USE!

Chapter 5

Better Marksmanship

CARRY POSITION, WELL BALANCED

MIDDLE OF SWING

**K**EEP LEFT HAND ON FORE-END AND RAISE. THE RIGHT HAND COMES ACROSS AND GRABS THE GRIP. FINISH THE SWING WITH GUN BUTT AGAINST THE SHOULDER AND THE SLING IS IN PLACE ON THE LEFT UPPER ARM. GUN LINES UP NATURALLY-- READY TO SHOOT!

# EXCESS WAVERINGS

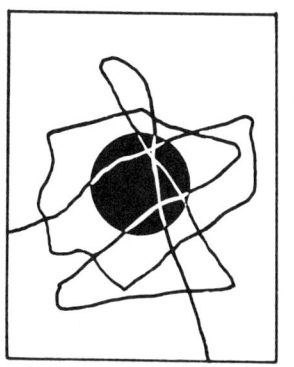

**W**ITHOUT PRACTICE, YOUR RIFLE'S FRONT SIGHT IS LIKELY TO WAVER ALL OVER THE TARGET AS YOU TRY TO HOLD IT STEADY FOR THE TRIGGER SQUEEZE AS SHOWN ABOVE.

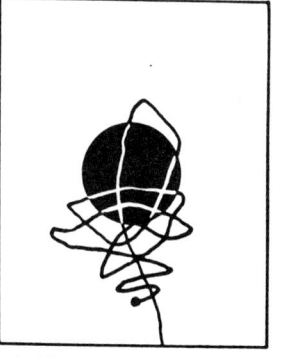

Chapter 5

Better Marksmanship

**P**RACTICE SIGHTING A FEW MINUTES A DAY OR 2 OR 3 TIMES A WEEK DURING THE SUMMER TO IMPROVE YOUR ACTUAL SHOOTING ON THE RANGE. FIX A SMALL TARGET ON A WALL AND AFTER A COUPLE OF WEEKS' PRACTICE YOU'LL FIND LESS WAVER AS IS SHOWN IN THE LOWER CHART.

**T**AKE A DEEP BREATH THEN EXHALE TO NATURAL AND AIM.

**Chapter 5**

Better Marksmanship

# SIMPLE EXERCISE FOR MARKSMANSHIP

Here is one that after two or three weeks of 15 minutes' daily practice will greatly reduce waverings. First, practice holding an aim on a target for a minute at one time. Later, hang a weight on the barrel to practice with. After a few sessions you'll be able to hold for longer periods. When you think you're pretty good, aim without the weight. Your gun seems as light as a feather and the wavering is hardly noticable! And how your SHOTS improve!

Another tip: Get a good night's sleep before shooting!

# TAKE TIME TO AIM

Don't think you won't have time to properly aim at the startling or noisy targets before they get out of range or sight. This THOUGHT is responsible for more misses than hits!

Some hunters count, "One, two, three, etc.", to calm themselves into taking more time to aim. This also permits the shot pattern in spreading to cover a larger area making easier hits at longer distances. You won't blow game to pieces, either!

Chapter 5

Better Marksmanship

Chapter 5

Better Marksmanship

# HOT VERSUS COLD RIFLE BARRELS

WHAT'S GOIN' ON?

THAT'S A TARGET SHOOTER--WARMIN' HIS RIFLE--FOR US!

BANG! BANG! BING!

DIFFERENT BARREL VIBRATIONS RESULT FROM CHANGING BARREL TEMPERATURES. THUS, THE BULLET'S POINT OF IMPACT (WHERE IT HITS) CHANGES AS THE BARREL HEATS UP. AFTER SEVERAL SHOTS, BARREL HEAT REACHES A POINT WHERE THE VIBRATIONS AND ALL BULLET FLIGHTS ARE ALIKE. TARGET SHOOTERS ADJUST SIGHTS AFTER A WARM UP. A HUNTER SHOULD DELAY SHOTS WHEN SIGHTING-IN TO KEEP BARREL COOL AS IF IN HUNTING!

# HOW MUCH RECOIL?

Chapter 5

Better Marksmanship

**A** 12 GAUGE SHOTGUN WEIGHING 7½ POUNDS HAS A RECOIL OF 27.9 FT. POUNDS WHEN A SHELL HAVING 3¼ DRAMS OF POWDER AND 1⅛ OZ. OF SHOT IS USED. THIS HEAVY RECOIL (OR "KICK") IS NOT USUALLY FELT WHEN SHOOTING <u>OFFHAND</u> AT GAME BECAUSE, IN STANDING, A SHOOTER "ROLLS WITH THE PUNCH" WHEREAS, THE <u>PRONE</u> SHOT CAN'T.

**A** .375 MAGNUM CARTRIDGE IN A RIFLE WEIGHING 8 POUNDS 4 OZ. HAS <u>31.2</u> FOOT POUNDS RECOIL, LESS THAN 4 POUNDS MORE THAN THE 12 GAUGE YET MOST MEN CONSIDER IT TOO PUNISHING FOR THEM!

**A** .30-06 8 LB. RIFLE HAS ONLY 17.5 FT. POUNDS RECOIL YET TO SOME IT'S PUNISHING!

# DO YOU FLINCH WHEN YOU FIRE THAT NEW CANNON?

**Chapter 5**

Better Marksmanship

**W**ITHOUT REALIZING IT, PERHAPS YOU DO. MANY SHOOTERS DO AND NEVER KNOW IT.

**H**AVE A FRIEND LOAD IT BEHIND YOUR BACK EACH TIME BEFORE EACH SHOT IS FIRED. TELL HIM TO LEAVE IT EMPTY ON ONE YOU DON'T EXPECT. IF YOU JERK ON THE EMPTY, YOU'RE A FLINCHER.

**C**URE YOURSELF BY "DRY-FIRING" (NO LOADS). DAILY, PRACTICE PULLING THE TRIGGER ON IMAGINARY TARGETS, RELAXING BODY TENSION. INSTALL A GOOD RECOIL PAD. SWITCH TO A LIGHTER CALIBER FOR AWHILE IF NECESSARY.

# RECOIL CONSCIOUS? THESE ARE LIGHT KICKERS!

**Chapter 5**

Better Marksmanship

Rifles such as the light .250/3000 Savage and .257 are ideal for the "little woman" because the recoil of either is light and both will handle deer-size game and black bears.

The .22 Hornet has 0.7 foot pounds of recoil, the .220 Swift has 4.7, a .257 has 6.9, a .250/3000 about the same and a .30-30 has 9 ft. pounds.

These rifles have a bit more; a .300 Savage has 11 ft. pounds and a .270 has 14.3, yet many women shoot these as well as the .30-06 at its 17.5!

**.22** and .220; for varmints only!

# HOW TO BORE SIGHT A RIFLE AND SAVE ON AMMUNITION...

Chapter 5

Better Marksmanship

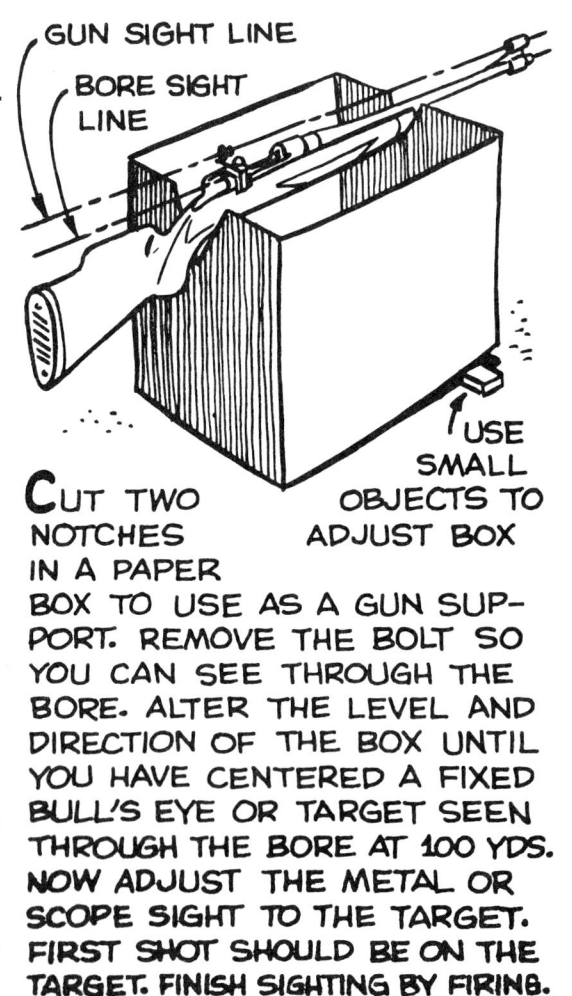

GUN SIGHT LINE

BORE SIGHT LINE

USE SMALL OBJECTS TO ADJUST BOX

Cut two notches in a paper box to use as a gun support. Remove the bolt so you can see through the bore. Alter the level and direction of the box until you have centered a fixed bull's eye or target seen through the bore at 100 yds. Now adjust the metal or scope sight to the target. First shot should be on the target. Finish sighting by firing.

# "SIGHTING IN" TIPS FOR A RIFLEMAN

**T**URN THE DIAGRAM SIDEWISE TO SEE WHERE A SCOPE SIGHTED RIFLE BULLET CROSSES LINE OF SIGHT.

**A**DJUST SCOPE TO BULLSEYE THE BULLET AT 25 YDS. NOTE THAT AT 25 YDS. 4 CLICKS IN ADJUSTMENT EQUAL 1 CLICK AT 100 YDS. ON THE PAPER. NOW AT 100 YDS., ADJUST TO NEEDS.

**U**SING <u>IRON</u> SIGHTS, SHOOT FIRST AT <u>12 ½</u> YDS. MAKE 8 CLICKS PER ¼ INCH (RECEIVER TYPE SIGHT), THEN 1 CLICK AT 100 YDS.

Chapter 5

Better Marksmanship

LINE OF SIGHT (AIM).

BULLET'S PATH -- FIRST CROSSES LINE OF SIGHT AT 25 YDS. IT THEN RISES TO...

...DROP, CROSSING LINE OF SIGHT AGAIN (ON TARGET) AT 100 YDS.

HORIZON

Chapter 5

Better Marksmanship

# FIELD SHOOTING SAFETY TIPS......

SET UP YOUR TARGET IN FRONT OF AN EMBANKMENT OR STEEP HILL TO ACT AS A BACKSTOP.

AVOID THIS!

RICOCHET

DON'T USE A STONY HILL OR A SHALLOW HILL THAT BULLETS WILL RICOCHET FROM. YOU HAVE NO CONTROL OVER WILD BULLETS THAT CAN BE DEADLY.

AVOID ANY LOCATION WHERE A HIGH SHOT CAN MISS THE BACKSTOP. A .22 CALIBER LONG RIFLE BULLET CAN CARRY 5,100 FT. IF BARREL IS ELEVATED AT A 33° ANGLE. DRY SAND OR GRASS-COVERED LOAM ARE GOOD BULLET STOPPERS!

# A PRACTICE TARGET FOR BIG GAME......

**Chapter 5**

**Better Marksmanship**

BOUNCING PATH OF TARGET

ENBANKMENT OR HILL

PAPER CARDBOARD

**A**LTERNATE WITH A FRIEND ROLLING AN OLD AUTO TIRE DOWN A HILL AND SHOOTING AT A SQUARE OF CARDBOARD FITTED INSIDE. SELECT A LOCATION WITH A HILL FOR THE BULLET BACKSTOP FOR SAFETY. THE ROLLING, BOUNCING TARGET SIMULATES LIVE GAME IN ACTION.

# TEST FIRING A SHOTGUN WILL AID YOU TO BETTER RESULTS

Chapter 5

Better Marksmanship

THE BEST WAY OF <u>KNOWING</u> WHAT SORT OF A PATTERN YOUR GUN WILL SHOOT IS TO TEST FIRE IT AT A LARGE (5 OR 6 FT. SQUARE) PIECE OF PAPER FROM 40 YARDS. DIFFERENT SHOT PATTERNS WILL BE HAD WITH DIFFERENT SIZE SHOT. FIND THE SIZES IT SHOOTS THE MOST EVENLY INTO A 30 INCH CIRCLE. FIRE SEVERAL OF EACH SIZE FOR CONCLUSIVE RESULTS.

# WHAT DOES CHOKE PATTERN PER CENT MEAN IN SHOTGUNS?

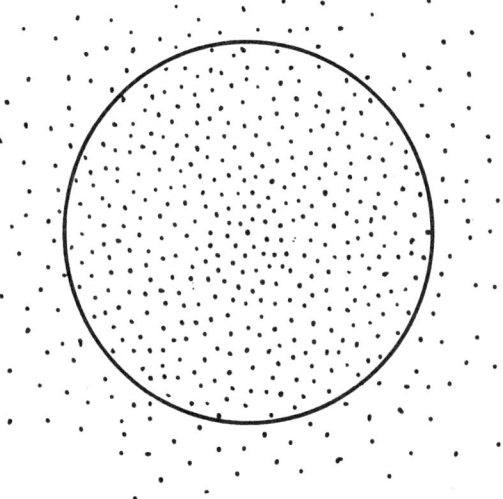

Chapter 5

Better Marksmanship

If 322 PELLETS OUT OF A REG. 12 GA. LOAD OF 460 NUMBER 8'S STRIKE <u>INSIDE</u> A 30 IN. CIRCLE AT 40 YDS., IT'S A <u>70%</u> PATTERN OR FULL CHOKE. A 12 GA. MODIFIED CHOKE PUTS ABOUT 276 OR <u>60%</u> OF THE SHOT IN THE CIRCLE--A 60% PATTERN. IMPROVED CYLINDER--45 TO 50%, A FULL CYLINDER (WITH NO CHOKE)--30 TO 35%.

FULL CHOKE: LONG SHOTS.
FULL CYLINDER: SHORTS.

# PRACTICE WING SHOTS WITH CLAY PIGEONS

**Chapter 5**

**Better Marksmanship**

Not one gunner in a hundred can start out on "opening day" feeling sure of his swing, target leading, and poise, unless he has done some shooting since the last season. Team up with a pal to share shots and throws, using a hand trap and clay pigeons for practice. It will pay off on opening day!

# WING-SHOT TIPS FOR BEGINNERS...

To BECOME A GOOD WING-SHOT DEMANDS A LOT OF SHOOTING PRACTICE AT ACTUAL FLYING TARGETS! TODAY'S LIMITED BIRDS ARE NOT THE SOLUTION. SKEET OR HAND TRAP CLAY TARGETS RESEMBLE UPLAND GAME BIRDS THE BEST.

SOME BIRDS GET UNDER WAY SO QUICKLY THAT THEY HAVE LEVELED OFF BEFORE THE GUNNER HAS COLLECTED HIS WITS. THUS, THE GUNNER MUST SWING AHEAD OF A BIRD BEFORE FIRING OR A MISS WILL RESULT.

OTHER RISING BIRDS SEEM TO PAUSE A BIT IN LEVELING OFF BEFORE "POURING ON THE COAL"! THIS MOMENT (AS ABOVE) OFFERS THE EASIEST TARGET ON RISING BIRDS. BE QUICK BUT COOL!

Chapter 5

Better Marksmanship

# A WING SHOOTER'S FOOTWORK.........

**Chapter 5**

**Better Marksmanship**

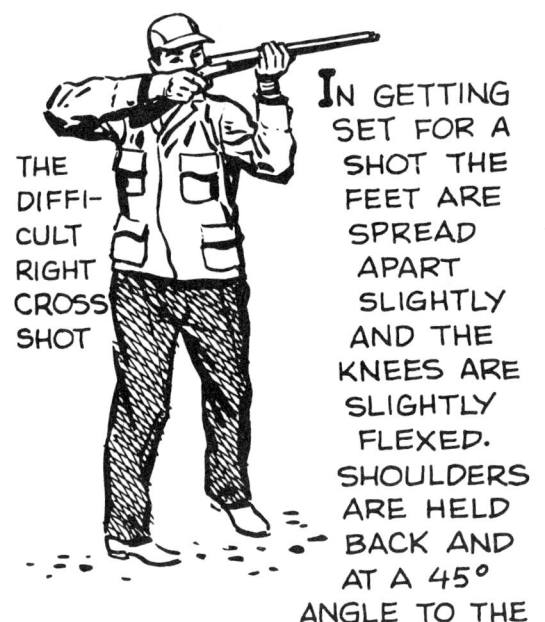

THE DIFFICULT RIGHT CROSS SHOT

IN GETTING SET FOR A SHOT THE FEET ARE SPREAD APART SLIGHTLY AND THE KNEES ARE SLIGHTLY FLEXED. SHOULDERS ARE HELD BACK AND AT A 45° ANGLE TO THE BORE OF THE GUN. THE HEAD AND BACK ARE HELD ERECT WHILE THE GUN IS MOUNTED.

THE PREPARATIONS COMPLETED, THE BODY BEGINS TO PIVOT FROM THE WAIST <u>DOWN</u> TO THE FEET IN FOLLOWING A CROSSING TARGET. THE UPPER BODY PARTS REMAIN FIXED BUT RELAXED.

SHIFT YOUR WEIGHT IN TURNING ON THE BALLS OF YOUR FEET.

# CO-ORDINATION PAYS IN SNAP SHOOTING!

So called <u>NATURALLY</u> GOOD "SNAP SHOTS" COMBINE ALL THOUGHTS INTO ONE FAST ACTION KNOWINGLY OR NOT. YOU MAY ALSO MASTER THIS. PRACTICE BY: ① PIVOTING, OR LOCATING FEET WHILE ② POINTING GUN AS IT IS RAISED TO THE SHOULDER, ③ PULLING THE TRIGGER. IN THIS MANNER ONLY THE <u>ONE</u> DECISION TO SHOOT IS MADE INSTEAD OF THREE SEPARATE DECISIONS. IF YOU PRACTICE ENOUGH, YOU CAN BE EVEN FASTER!

Chapter 5

Better Marksmanship

**Chapter 5**

**Better Marksmanship**

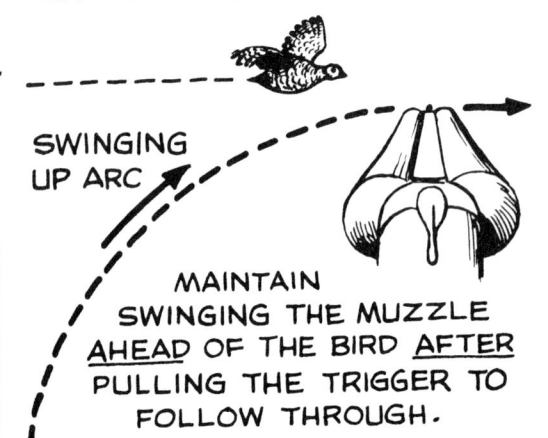

**"POINTING OUT"** IS THE NEXT STEP IN WING SHOOTING AFTER MASTERING SNAP SHOTS. THE DIFFERENCE BEGINS AS YOU SWING UP THE GUN.

SWINGING UP ARC

MAINTAIN SWINGING THE MUZZLE AHEAD OF THE BIRD AFTER PULLING THE TRIGGER TO FOLLOW THROUGH.

Begin swinging the gun's muzzle equal to the bird's flight speed but in front of or "leading" the bird as gun is raised towards the shoulder. As gun muzzle arcs upward to the level of flight, initiate pressure on the trigger and the eye tells the mind to keep the muzzle in front of the bird.

You may practice by "dry firing" (no live shells) at sparrows, etc.

# NO. 1 TECHNIQUE OF FORWARD ALLOWANCE

SWING EQUALS TARGET SPEED

Chapter 5

Better Marksmanship

Gun-muzzle swings at a sustained speed equal to but in front of the target. On high angle or open targets, there is enough time for deliberate calculation as to how far ahead the gun must be before firing. Experience by trial and error is the best teacher here.

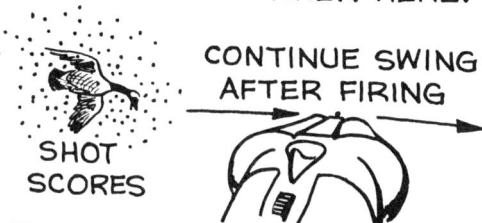

CONTINUE SWING AFTER FIRING

SHOT SCORES

The term "FORWARD ALLOWANCE", coined by Britons, describes best the later and present American term of "LEADING."

The "NO. 1 TECHNIQUE" is best for high flying ducks, etc.

# NO. 2 TECHNIQUE OF FORWARD ALLOWANCE

Chapter 5

Better Marksmanship

Gun-muzzle swings fast from BEHIND the target and is fired after passing it the right distance. Some FASTER swinging gunners prefer to shoot just as the muzzle passes the target WITHOUT SLOWING THEIR SWING. Never halt ANY swing.

CONTINUE SWING AFTER FIRING

The "NO. 2 TECHNIQUE" is ideal for quick, close range shots for upland game-birds at 20 to 35 yards. Skeet shooting is similar to upland game-bird shooting so it offers the best training and practice for this technique.

# NO. 3 TECHNIQUE OF FORWARD ALLOWANCE

GUN SWINGS UP WITHOUT "LEADING"

Chapter 5

Better Marksmanship

This technique is commonly known as snap-shooting. It is used only for unexpected emergency shots without time for the more reliable No. 2 technique.

The gun-muzzle is swung upward to intercept in front of the target. Gun is fired at the instant the muzzle is lined-up. A definite help is to arc the up-swing as in "pointing out" on crossing targets.

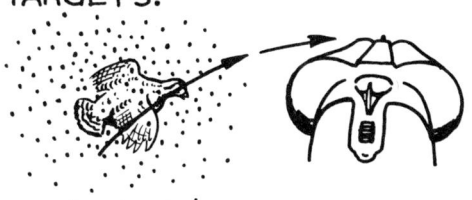

# RIFLES AND SHOTGUNS

Gun lovers, whether they hunt or not, find great pleasure in viewing and handling a fine gun. Some collectors invest considerable amounts of money in extensive arrays of rare and historic guns.

Today's modern rifles and shotguns range in price from a few dollars for single shot pieces, to several hundreds for the finest custom jobs. If you don't know much about rifles or shotguns when you are buying one, choose a new gun if you can afford it. It carries a factory guarantee and will give many years of excellent service. Don't buy a second-hand gun unless you know a bit about such things as its head space, strength of action, barrels, etc., or at least unless you can thoroughly depend upon the seller and the price.

The best place to buy is from a reputable local dealer, a department store, or a mail-order firm. The new gun should be in a factory carton with the factory grease and tags on it. All new guns are priced the same, so be certain it is in a new unhandled condition.

The gun should be cleaned after use and exposure to weather. Handling with sweaty hands may result in corrosion unless the gun is wiped with a cloth afterward. All oil should be removed from the barrel and chamber before a gun is fired, for safety's sake and to prevent excessive wear and pressure. Oily chamber walls prevent the shell from holding to the sides when it is fired, causing a greater backward thrust to bear upon the bolt or breech block.

Without going into the merits of various types of gun actions, let us say that a shotgun owner is well equipped for big game when using rifle slugs at ranges of less than 100 yards. Many deer hunters prefer it when on a stand in heavy brush. But it has its limitations and is suitable only for certain types of hunting. Each rifle and shotgun has its limitations and that's why so many types and sizes are offered. Be sure yours conforms to the game, the country, and the law.

Chapter 6

Rifles and Shotguns

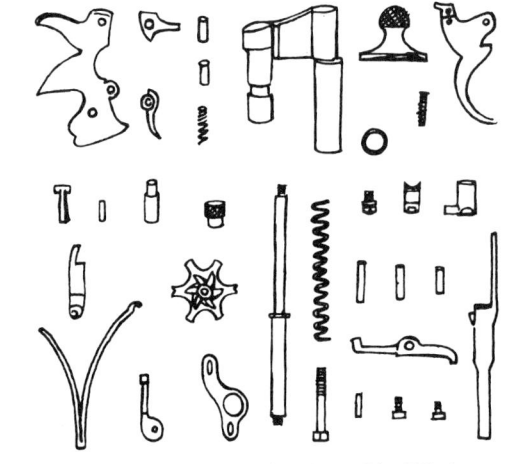

# DON'T TAKE A GUN APART CARELESSLY!

SOME OF THE "WORKS" OF A COLT OFFICIAL POLICE .38

EACH PART OF A HANDGUN, SHOTGUN OR RIFLE WAS DESIGNED BY EXPERTS FOR A PRECISE REASON. SOME GUNS ARE MORE COMPLEX THAN OTHERS. SCREWS ARE ELIMINATED WHENEVER POSSIBLE BECAUSE THEY WORK LOOSE, RUST OR BREAK. PINS WORK OUT AND USUALLY ARE COVERED BY OTHER PARTS TO PREVENT IT. ONE SPRING OR CATCH MAY HOLD EVERYTHING TOGETHER. IF YOU DON'T KNOW HOW TO DO IT, TAKE IT TO A GUNSMITH.

# CHOOSE THE RIGHT TYPE OF BULLET...

**Chapter 6**

Rifles and Shotguns

A HEAVY <u>ROUND</u> NOSE BULLET IS BEST FOR HUNTING IN BRUSHY WOODS. THE LOWER VELOCITY OF HEAVY (180 TO 300 GRAIN) ROUND NOSE BULLETS OR RIFLED SHOTGUN SLUGS PENETRATES THE BRUSH BEST AND IS DEFLECTED LESS BY TWIGS, ETC. IN FLIGHT TO THE MARK. CHOOSE THE HEAVIEST BULLET YOUR GUN WILL SHOOT.

LIGHTER, HIGHER VELOCITY, <u>POINTED</u> NOSE BULLETS ARE THE BEST FOR LONG SHOTS.

# "CALIBER .30, M-1" IS NOT A ".30-30"!

Chapter 6
Rifles and Shotguns

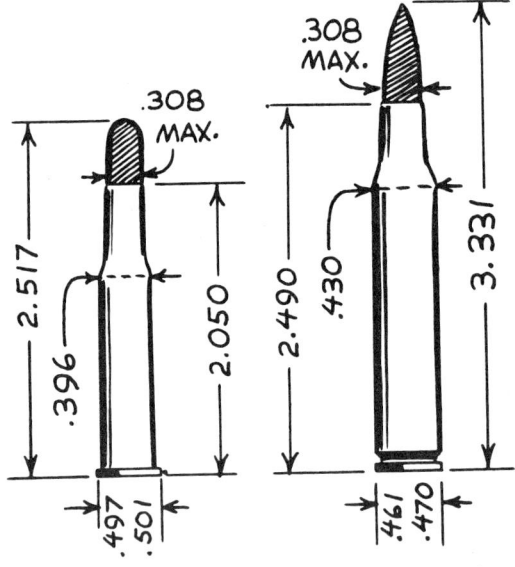

.30-30    .30-06

**M**ANY SPORTSMEN CONFUSE THESE TWO! THE ".30-30" WAS DESIGNED FOR THE MODEL 1894 WINCHESTER LEVER ACTION RIFLE, TESTING AROUND 39,000 LBS. THE ".30, M-1," ".30, M-2," ".30 U.S. GOV'T.," AND ".30-06" ARE ALL THE SAME. TODAY, ONLY BOLT ACTIONS ARE MADE IN THE U.S.A. FOR .30-06'S 50,000 LB. PRESSURE.

160

# SPITZER BULLETS ARE DANGEROUS IN TUBE MAGAZINES

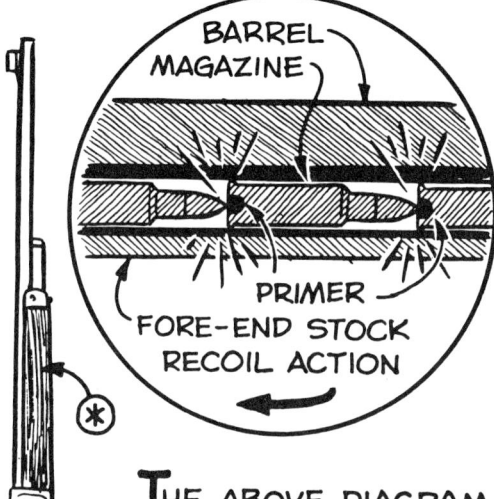

Chapter 6

Rifles and Shotguns

BARREL
MAGAZINE
PRIMER
FORE-END STOCK RECOIL ACTION

The above diagram shows how jarring recoil can fire a cartridge when the primer is struck by a spitzer or sharp-pointed bullet. Such bullets are to be used ONLY in bolt actions or in lever actions having a rotary magazine.

Winchester's Model 71, tubular type, (✱) is shown above.

# DANGEROUS HEAD SPACE IN A GUN

*Chapter 6*

*Rifles and Shotguns*

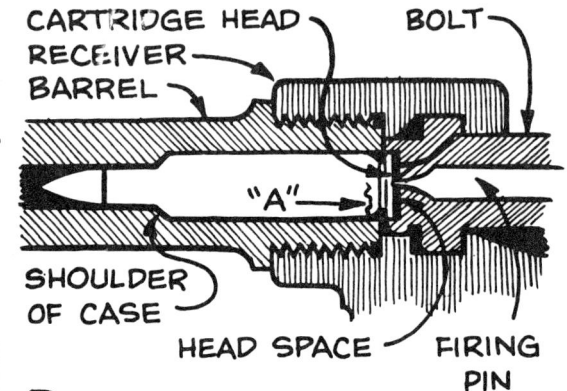

Labels on diagram: CARTRIDGE HEAD, RECEIVER, BARREL, BOLT, "A", SHOULDER OF CASE, HEAD SPACE, FIRING PIN

Diagram of a cartridge in the breech of a Mauser bolt action is shown above.

Through wear or sloppy manufacturing, excessive space between the face of the bolt and cartridge head may exist when a cartridge case is too short or when the case chamber is too long. In firing, the firing pin drives the case forward before the primer fires the load. The first pressure locks the case walls to the chamber. Still expanding, the head moving too far back to the face, may separate at "A".

# TEST FOR TRIGGER PULL WEIGHT......

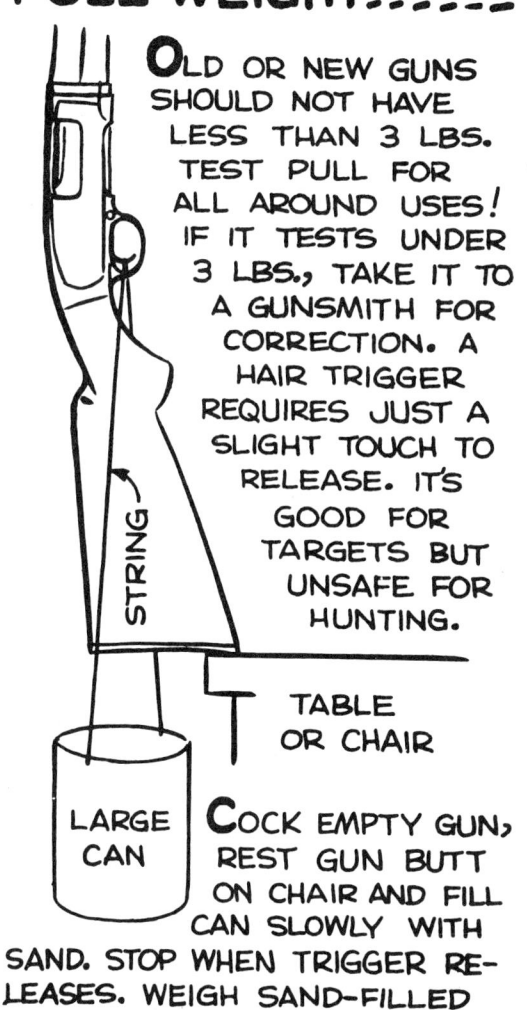

**O**LD OR NEW GUNS SHOULD NOT HAVE LESS THAN 3 LBS. TEST PULL FOR ALL AROUND USES! IF IT TESTS UNDER 3 LBS., TAKE IT TO A GUNSMITH FOR CORRECTION. A HAIR TRIGGER REQUIRES JUST A SLIGHT TOUCH TO RELEASE. IT'S GOOD FOR TARGETS BUT UNSAFE FOR HUNTING.

STRING

TABLE OR CHAIR

LARGE CAN

**C**OCK EMPTY GUN, REST GUN BUTT ON CHAIR AND FILL CAN SLOWLY WITH SAND. STOP WHEN TRIGGER RELEASES. WEIGH SAND-FILLED CAN FOR EXACT TRIGGER PULL.

Chapter 6

Rifles and Shotguns

Chapter 6
Rifles and Shotguns

# HOODED ROUND BEAD SIGHTS......

HOODLESS ROUND BEAD BECOMES INDISTINCT IN SUNLIGHT WHEN SIGHTED IN.

← CENTER LINE OF TARGET
← BULL'S-EYE.
CENTER LINE OF SIGHT

WHEN SHOOTING UNDER OPPOSITE LIGHTING CONDITIONS THAN WERE USED FOR SIGHTING IN, THE RESULT MAY BE AN ERROR OF SEVERAL INCHES AT 100 YARDS.

A HOOD PREVENTS DISTORTION AND PROTECTS THE BEAD. IF IT PERFECTLY CENTERS THE BEAD, IT AIDS IN FAST SIGHTING. SOME AUTHORITIES DISLIKE THIS USE BUT I'M FOR IT.!

BEAD

# FLAT-TOPPED POST FRONT SIGHTS.....

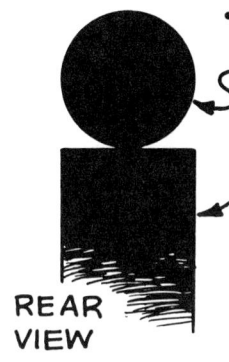

TARGET BULL'S-EYE SHOULD REST ON TOP OF THE FLAT TOP POST SIGHT.

REAR VIEW

ADJUST THE REAR SIGHT SO THE SHOT WILL CENTER IN THE BULL'S-EYE WHEN SIGHTED IN AS ABOVE.

ANOTHER FLAT TOP POST SIGHT WITH A SQUARE BEAD ON A SLANT TO COLLECT LIGHT UNDER POOR CONDITIONS IS SHOWN BELOW IN A 3/4 REAR VIEW. SIGHT IN EXACTLY AS ABOVE.

SLANTED BEAD

BOTH SIGHTS ARE RUGGED AND ACCURATE.

YOU CANNOT FIND A BETTER IRON SIGHT FOR HUNTING.

**Chapter 6**

Rifles and Shotguns

# DOUBLE-BARREL VS. THE SINGLE....

**Chapter 6**
Rifles and Shotguns

DOUBLE-BARREL SHOTGUNS ARE EXCELLENT UPLAND GAME GUNS! MOST OF THIS IS CLOSE RANGE SHOOTING. SIDE-BY-SIDE BARRELS FORM A BROAD SIGHTING-PLANE FOR A MORE NEARLY SUBCONSCIOUS ALIGNMENT FOR QUICK SHOTS. TAPE WRAPPING OR A CHOKE DEVICE ON THE MUZZLE OF A SINGLE-BARREL ACHIEVES A LIKE RESULT.

LONG, SINGLE-BARREL GUNS WITH A SLENDER SIGHTING-PLANE IS BEST FOR A <u>PRECISE</u> ALIGNMENT ON HIGH OR LONG RANGE SHOTS AT DUCKS, ETC. <u>OVER</u> <u>AND</u> <u>UNDER</u> DOUBLES OFFER THIS SAME FEATURE.

# SHOTGUN "FEEL" TIPS

**I**F IT <u>FEELS</u> TOO LIGHT AND UNSTEADY IN CONTROL, YOU NEED A HEAVIER GUN OR LONGER BARRELS.

Chapter 6

Rifles and Shotguns

**I**F YOU DON'T LOOK <u>STRAIGHT</u> <u>DOWN</u> <u>THE</u> <u>BARREL</u> WHEN YOUR CHEEK IS FIRM ON THE COMB, THE COMB SHOULD BE LOWERED OR RAISED.

**I**F IT <u>FEELS</u> SLUGGISH AND SWINGS TOO SLOWLY, IT IS MUZZLE HEAVY AND PERHAPS ITS BARRELS ARE TOO LONG.

# "DROP" AND "PITCH" OF A SHOTGUN

**Chapter 6**

Rifles and Shotguns

WALL OR LINE OF SIGHT PLANE

COMB DROP 1½"

HEEL DROP 2½"

**G**RASP GUN GRIP, RAISE LOWER ARM FORMING A RIGHT ANGLE AT THE ELBOW. PLACE GUN BUTT AGAINST THE ARM TO FIT FROM BENT TRIGGER FINGER TO UPPER ARM. GUN SHOWN IS A WINCHESTER MODEL 12. IT FITS THE AVERAGE MAN. A TALLER MAN MAY NEED A PAD FOR MORE LENGTH OR A SHORT MAN LESS LENGTH.

**S**TOCK LENGTH OF PULL: FROM TRIGGER TO BUTT CENTER.

TOE

FLOOR

# "DROP" AND "PITCH" OF A SHOTGUN

2¼" PITCH

**D**ROP AND PITCH GO TOGETHER. PITCH CONTROLS MOSTLY SHOOTING HIGH OR LOW, IF THE COMB FITS THE CHEEK AND THE BUTT FITS THE SHOULDER. PITCH FOR WATERFOWL IS BETWEEN 2¼" TO 2½". FOR UPLAND GAME IT IS 1¾" TO 2". IF YOU CONSISTENTLY UNDERSHOOT, THE PITCH SHOULD BE LESSENED. OVER- SHOOTING, IT IS INCREASED. IN NATURAL SIGHTING YOU SHOULD NOT SEE TOO MUCH OR TOO LITTLE OF THE BARREL.

WALL

BREECH TOUCHES

HEEL AND TOE AGAINST THE FLOOR.

Chapter 6

Rifles and Shotguns

Chapter 6
Rifles and Shotguns

# "DROP" AND "PITCH"

Test your shotgun fit as you would hastily swing for a fast shot. That is, with the cheek firm against the comb but not as hard as you might press with more shooting time.

Using this sketch for a guide, identify your gun's fit, then check the answers below.

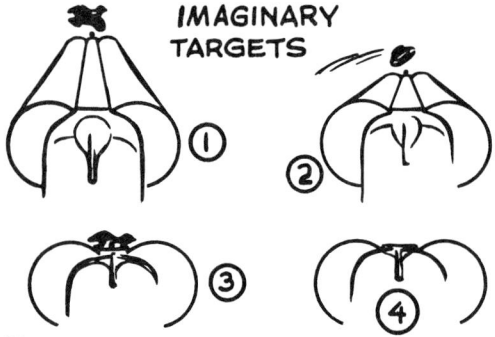

IMAGINARY TARGETS

①TOO MUCH BARREL, COMB IS TOO HIGH. RESULTS IN OVERSHOOTING. REMEDY: CUT DOWN COMB A BIT.

②CORRECT, HASTY BUT FIRM.

③CORRECT, DELIBERATE, HARD.

④WRONG. BEAD AND TARGET ARE LOST. REMEDY: BUILD UP COMB HEIGHT WITH A SLEEVE.

# CARE OF EQUIPMENT

Whether your equipment is **inexpensive** or costly, it will give longer **service** with proper care. Binoculars are one accessory that should never be handled carelessly. A fine pair may cost more than your pet gun, and only a slight bump or jarring can put it out of alignment. Like binoculars, much of your equipment varies in price according to the quality. Less expensive, **serviceable** items should be given the **same** care as your other gear.

If you neglect occasional inspection of your firearms, clothing, tent, etc., corrosion, rust or moths will soon force replacement. On the other hand, if you treat these items carefully they will give long service. Then, instead of constant replacement you can add other equipment. For example, fine woolen hunting socks should be worn only once between washings. It's best to take several pairs of socks to camp so that enough time can be allowed for drying. Even in a warm cabin, **socks** may require more than one day for drying. I have known of hunters wearing one pair of socks day after day without washing them until holes and sore, tired feet resulted.

Rubber air mattresses are a great improvement over a bough bed, because of the time it takes to make a good bough bed. But even with the best care a rubber air mattress will last only a few seasons, and much less time when neglected.

Sleeping bags should be designed so they may be opened wide for airing whenever possible, preferably every day. Right here, I'd like to advise against purchasing any so-called feather (not water fowl down) bag. It will cost as much or more than a wool-lined one, and is cold except for semi-tropical or warm-weather camping. Such bags need extra wool blankets in cold weather. You are better off, therefore, with a light canvas cover and blankets from home.

# CLEAN A RIFLE OF DIRT OR SNOW IN A JIFFY WITHOUT A CLEANING ROD

**Chapter 7**

Care of Equipment

This can happen to you away from camp. You stumble or fall and your rifle is full of dirt or snow. By all means never fire your rifle until all matter is removed!

Unload gun, tap or shake out as much as possible. Then blow through the breach to the muzzle of the bore. Now fire a primed cartridge after first removing the bullet and powder. It safely finishes the job. You might carry a primed empty for such use.

**Chapter 7**
Care of Equipment

# ARE GUN LUBRICANTS NECESSARY........?

**N**O LUBRICANT MAY BE NECESSARY IN THE WINTER FOR THE AVERAGE USER. IN FACT, IN VERY COLD WEATHER OILS STIFFEN AND SLOW DOWN THE GUN'S ACTION. IN SUCH CASES, IT IS BETTER WITHOUT <u>ANY</u> OIL.

**S**UMMERTIME LUBRICANTS MAY BE SATISFACTORY IF DIRT IS NO PROBLEM, BUT HERE AGAIN IT IS NOT NECESSARY FOR THE AVERAGE USER.

**I**T <u>IS</u> ADVISABLE AFTER CLEANING TO LIGHTLY OIL THE OUTER SURFACES TO PROTECT AGAINST RUST, HANDLING, ETC., OR WHEN IT IS STORED IN GREASE AT THE END OF THE SEASON.

**S**ILICONE OR GRAPHITE MAY BE USED IF YOUR GUN OIL IS STIFF.

# CORROSION (RUST) PREVENTING TIPS

**Chapter 7**

Care of Equipment

Guns may be wiped dry or mildly heated dry and still retain an invisible film of water. Unprotected iron or steel exposed to air and water will oxidize and rust. Therefore when guns are to be stored, the water film must be replaced with a protective oil film.

Cosmoline is used for storing military firearms. It is a commercial grade of petroleum jelly. Petroleum jelly is available in any drug store.

White Russian mineral oil (for internal human use) is acid free and non-corrosive. It's a good gun lubricant.

**Chapter 7**

Care of Equipment

# USING GUN COVERS

Flannel or fleece lined covers or cases are excellent protectors of a gun's finish and sights enroute to and from your shooting grounds. Unprotected rubbing against an automobile's upholstery results in wearing off the gun blue to invite rust and corrosion. Uncased guns rubbing together causes dents and scratches.

Cased guns should <u>NEVER</u> be loaded!

Where climate may cause metal parts to sweat (condensation) in a room, it is best to store guns uncased so that circulating air helps to keep them dry!

Oil stored guns lightly.

# TIPS FOR STORING AMMUNITION.........

**F**IRST, LET'S DISCARD THE NOTION THAT ONLY FRESH AMMUNITION IS DEPENDABLE!

**A** WOODEN BOX SERVES NICELY AS A CONTAINER FOR MIXED-SIZED SHELL AND CARTRIDGE CARTONS. IF KEPT IN A DRY, HEAT-FREE CLOSET (AVOIDING CELLARS AND ATTICS), YOUR VALUABLE AND SOMETIMES SCARCE "AMMO" WILL KEEP INDEFINITELY!

**S**HAKING A POWDER CAN BUILDS UP STATIC ELECTRICITY. DON'T DO IT!

**K**EEP POWDER CAN TIGHTLY CORKED, DRY AND HEAT FREE!

Chapter 7

Care of Equipment

# SAFE STORAGE OF OUTDOOR GEAR....

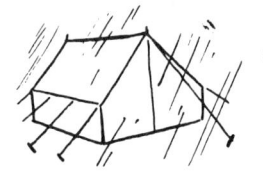

**Chapter 7**
**Care of Equipment**

**A** WET TENT SHOULD BE DRIED BEFORE STORING FOR ANY LENGTH OF TIME OR ELSE IT MILDEWS QUICKLY. IF IT MUST BE BROUGHT HOME DAMP, SET IT UP TO DRY AS SOON AS POSSIBLE. CLEAN, ROLL LOOSELY AND STORE IN A COOL, DRY PLACE OFF GROUND.

**L**EAVE A LITTLE AIR IN A RUBBER AIR MATTRESS AND ROLL OR FOLD LOOSELY (NEVER TIGHT) TO PREVENT CRACKING. STORE IN A COOL PLACE (NOT ATTICS).

**C**LEAN DOWN OR WOOL GARMENTS, SLEEPING BAGS, ETC., BEFORE PACKING HEAVILY WITH MOTH BALLS OR FLAKES IN A TIGHT BOX.

**S**ADDLE SOAP LEATHER BOOTS, ETC. STORE IN COOL, DRY PLACE.

## STORAGE CARE OF STOVE, LAMPS, ETC.

**R**emove soot from wood-burning tent stoves and pipes, then oil lightly. Soot collects moisture to cause rust quickly!

*Chapter 7*

*Care of Equipment*

**C**lean off grease on burners of gasoline or oil stoves. Touch up with oil where enamel is chipped off. Empty and rinse tank insides with clean fuel to remove tiny bits of sediment that would clog generator when used again. Oil leather (or glycerin dip rubber) pump plunger.

**F**lush and drain tank, treat pump plunger of pressure lamps as with stove above. Dry storage for both.

**C**lean and grease axes and shovels. Oil knives.

Chapter 7

Care of Equipment

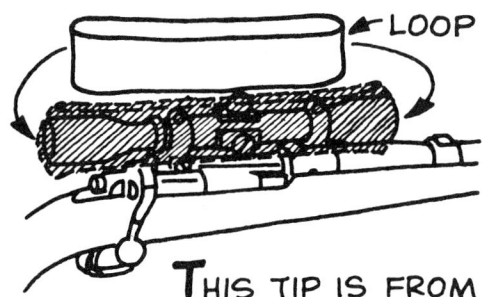

# SCOPE LENS COVER
— FOR DUST, RAIN OR SNOW —
Cut an old rubber innertube into loops 1½" to 2" wide.

← LOOP

This tip is from the "DOPE BAG" panel of experts in the "AMERICAN RIFLE-MAN" magazine by the famous ELMER KEITH, big game guide, hunter and author.

Stretch a loop lengthwise on the scope to protect the lens from rain or snow. For a quick shot, pull the back loop end free of the lens and let go. Its flight leaves the sight ready for instant action. Carry extra loops in a pocket for replacements.

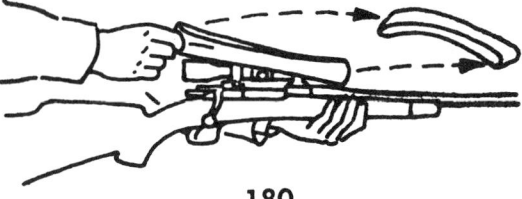

# BINOCULAR TIPS...

Chapter 7

Care of Equipment

If the vision looks this way, the glasses are not set to conform with the distance between your eyes. Adjust them by moving the hinge to bring the exit pupils of the glass closer together.

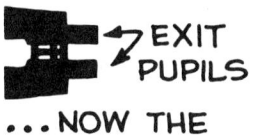

EXIT PUPILS

...Now the vision should look like this.

If two images are seen at once like ←this, the alignment is off and it needs repair.

**Chapter 7**

Care of Equipment

# BINOCULARS TIPS

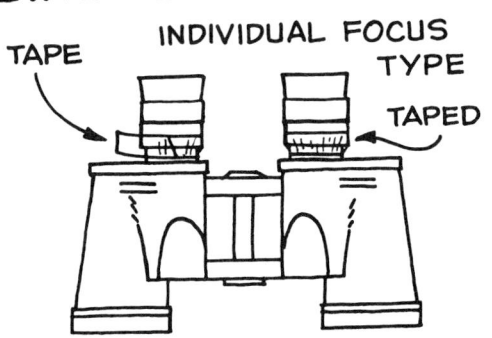

INDIVIDUAL FOCUS TYPE
TAPE
TAPED

**W**RAP TRANSPARENT 'SCOTCH' TAPE AROUND THE OCULAR FOCUS ADJUSTMENTS OF INDIVIDUAL FOCUS GLASSES OR BIND CENTER CONTROL OF CENTRAL FOCUSING GLASSES AFTER ADJUSTING THE FOCUS TO SUIT YOUR EYESIGHT. THIS PREVENTS AN ACCIDENTAL CHANGE OF EXACT ADJUSTMENT, SAVING PRECIOUS TIME WHEN YOU NEED THE GLASSES QUICKLY!

LOOP CARRY STRAP

**G**LASSES HUNG CASELESS ON A STRAP ARE PROTECTED AGAINST RAIN, ETC., WITH A THROW-AWAY LOOP CUT FROM AN OLD INNER-TUBE.

# CHECK BINOCULAR ALIGNMENT

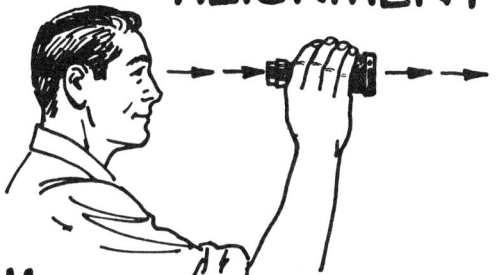

**Chapter 7**

Care of Equipment

**M**ISALIGNMENT RESULTS IN EYESTRAIN FROM FUSING TWO DIFFERENT IMAGES INTO ONE.

**W**HILE LOOKING AT A DISTANT HORIZONTAL ROOF TOP OR WALL, SLOWLY MOVE BINOCULARS TOWARD THE OBJECT WHILE PEERING INTENTLY WITH BOTH EYES. WITHIN TEN INCHES YOU WILL SEE TWO SEPARATE IMAGES.

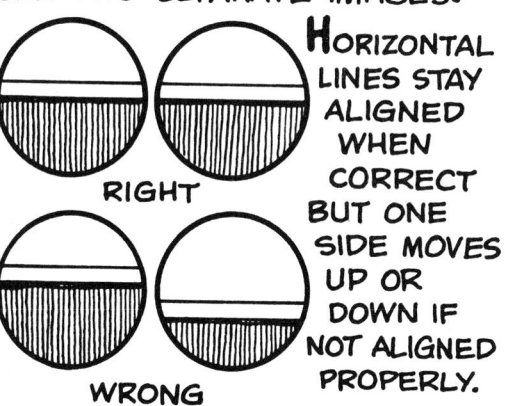

RIGHT

WRONG

**H**ORIZONTAL LINES STAY ALIGNED WHEN CORRECT BUT ONE SIDE MOVES UP OR DOWN IF NOT ALIGNED PROPERLY.

**Chapter 7**

*Care of Equipment*

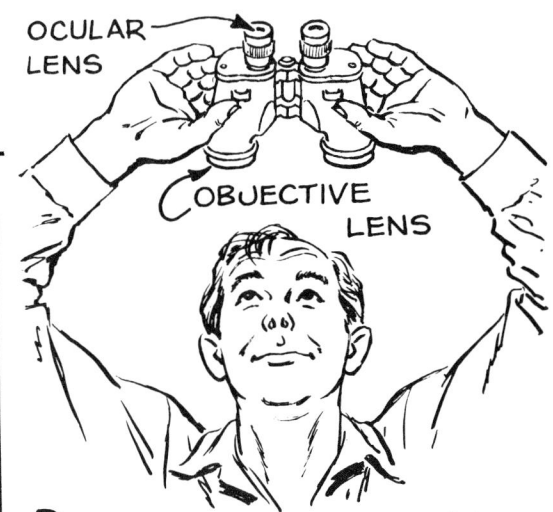

# CHECK BINOCULARS FOR CLEAN OPTICS

OCULAR LENS

OBJECTIVE LENS

Dust and moisture that settle on the inside surfaces of lens and prism reduces clear vision like dirt on a window. If present, particles are easily seen by <u>reversing</u> binoculars (ocular lens away from you) and looking skyward, objective lens 10 in. from your eyes. Do not take apart to clean inside. It's an expert's job, requiring realignment. Clean the outside lens with <u>clean</u> tissues after blowing off dust.

# TIP FOR THE QUICK USE OF BINOCULARS

THANKS TO **LT. JOHN DRAGGIE, U.S.N.** HATBORO, PA., WHO GIVES US THIS ONE!

Chapter 7

Care of Equipment

BINOCULARS, HANGING BY THE NECK STRAP, ARE PLACED IN-SIDE A ZIPPERED JACKET FRONT TO BE READY FOR IN-STANT USE BY PARTLY UNZIP-PING THE ZIPPER, THUS ELIMI-NATING THE FUMBLING WITH A CASE WHEN YOU'RE HURRIED OR POSSIBLE DANGER TO UNCASED GLASSES SWINGING ABOUT AS IN CLIMBING, ETC.

**Chapter 7**
Care of Equipment

# KNIFE SHARPENING

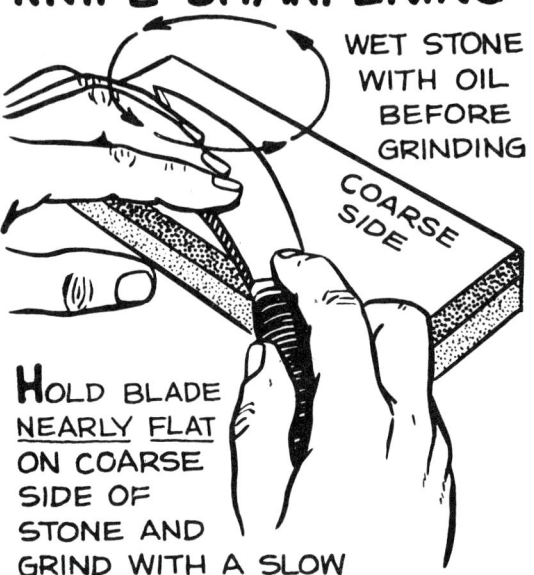

WET STONE WITH OIL BEFORE GRINDING

COARSE SIDE

Hold blade nearly flat on coarse side of stone and grind with a slow circular motion from tip to handle for about a minute then grind the other side. Repeat until blade tapers to a thin edge. Now turn the stone's fine side up, oil it and grind as before. When sharp, give it a keen edge by drawing it one direction only, away from the edge, for 50 or 60 strokes on each side. For razor sharpness, strop it on a razor strop, old belt or boot top!

Most new knives are dull!

# HOW TO DRY BOOTS

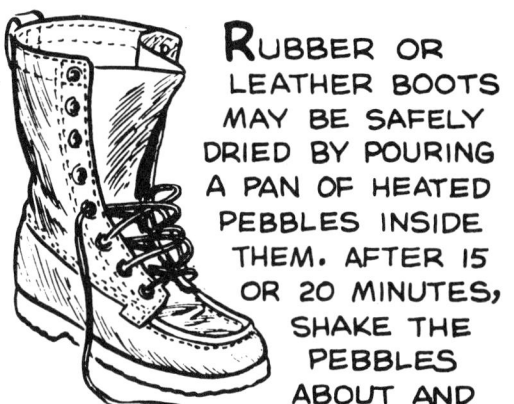

Rubber or leather boots may be safely dried by pouring a pan of heated pebbles inside them. After 15 or 20 minutes, shake the pebbles about and let them stand some more. Repeat until dry. When dry, apply neat's-foot oil to leather boots instantly.

Never dry boots as close to a fire as <u>this</u>!

Chapter 7

Care of Equipment

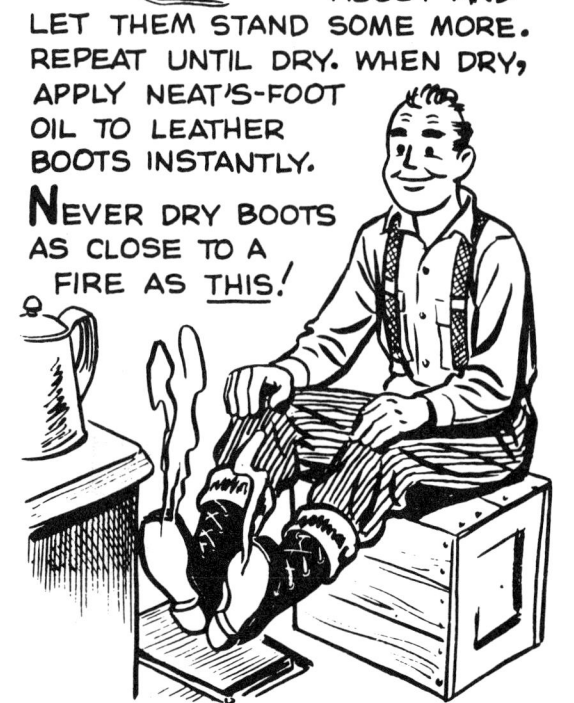

Chapter 7

Care of Equipment

# HUNTER'S CLOTHING FOR COLD WEATHER

FREE SWING BACK
(WOOL)

THIS SELECTION INSULATES TO KEEP YOU WARM WITHOUT CAUSING FATIGUE FROM TOO MUCH WEIGHT!

CHOOSE PART COTTON AND WOOL UNDERWEAR TO ABSORB PERSPIRATION AND PROVIDE WARMTH. TWO LIGHT WOOL SHIRTS, ONE IS EASY TO REMOVE IF IT'S TOO WARM. LIGHT OR HEAVY WOOL TROUSERS ARE QUIET AGAINST BRUSH. A <u>ROOMY</u> DOWN-LINED OR AN "ACTION-BACK" WOOL COAT THAT COVERS YOUR SEAT, WORN WITH A HOOD OR EAR FLAP CAP OF YOUR CHOICE. A FUR AND DOWN CAP IS IDEAL! SELECT FOOTWEAR ACCORDING TO REGION.

# WATER REPELLENTS FOR CLOTHING.....

**Chapter 7**

**Care of Equipment**

For wool clothing, dissolve 1 ounce of lanolin in 1 quart of white gasoline. Dip the garments and hang them out to dry, pulling them into shape as you hang them up. Occasionally, turn them upside down to prevent all of the solution running to the lower sides.

For cotton, dissolve 1 oz. of beeswax in 1 qt. of white gasoline. Brush it on lightly.

Waterproofing boots is one of the many uses for petroleum jelly.

# WATERPROOFING TENTS AND TARPS

Chapter 7
Care of Equipment

ERECT AND CLEAN TENT THEN APPLY SOLUTION WITH A LARGE BRUSH IN THE OPEN AIR.

Commercial waterproofing solutions may be used or make your own with this formula. Shave and melt 3/4 lb. of beeswax or paraffin. Beeswax is more pliable but is the costlier. Dissolve either one in a gallon of warmed turpentine or WHITE gasoline. Warm the solvent in a metal pail or can placed in a wash tub of HOT water. AVOID ANY FIRE! Change tub water to re-heat. Treat exteriors only. Solution kills grass!

# CAR TOP CARRIERS

*DON'T PACK IT SO HIGH!*

Chapter 7

Care of Equipment

For the average sportsman without a trailer or pick-up truck, a car top carrier may serve instead. Put the luggage, tent, sleeping bags, bedding, etc. on the carrier and heavy items, such as outboard motor etc. in the car's trunk. Don't pack it too high and be sure it is securely fastened to the top. Cover it with a "tarp" and bind tight with rope. Ideal for hauling trophies, like deer, also!

# YOUR DOG

A hunting dog need not be of registered ancestry to be valuable to the average sportsman. And the breed of a dog does not always make him a hunter. Some dogs, not popularly accepted as hunting breeds, occasionally make fine field animals. In some cases, too, a mixed-breed dog will prove equal to or better than a pure-bred for hunting purposes. For instance, bear and lion hounds frequently are of mixed breeds to give better performance in the field.

Nevertheless, in choosing your first dog, it's best to stick to accepted breeds. The price of a pedigreed dog will vary considerably, and usually you get what you pay for. If you buy a trained dog, be prepared to pay more. A champion's price is whatever his owner demands.

If you have an untrained pup, training him will require many practice sessions over a period of weeks and months. You can train him yourself, or you can hire a trainer. Usually, a good trainer is a specialist and his time is in great demand.

Here are some simple training tips:

Get to know your dog and be as considerate of him as of a friend.

Help him understand what his job is. He'll hunt better for you if you give him careful and correct training.

If you have a rough day afield, don't take it out on your dog. He will be as disappointed about it as you. And praise him after you have downed a bird or rabbit that he has started. He should be proud of you, too.

Don't be afraid to make a pet of him! He likes to be petted by you.

If your dog doesn't seem well, don't try to doctor him yourself. Take him to a veterinarian for the sake of his health and because such treatment is due a good dog.

## TOURING WITH YOUR DOG.......

**Chapter 8**
**Your Dog**

More than 3,500 hotels and motor courts in North America gladly accept guests with dogs. This is good news for those who wish to take their dogs when touring. A directory listing these hostelries may be had for 10 cents (postage & handling charge) by writing to the Gaines Dog Research Center, 250 Park Ave., New York 17, N.Y.

This copy, entitled "Touring with Towser," includes special conditions of some of the hostelries and helpful hints for traveling with your dog!

# PROTECTION FOR YOUR DOG FROM EXHAUST FUMES!

WRONG

DOG CRATE

Chapter 8

Your Dog

**S**PORTING DOGS SHOULD NEVER BE CARRIED IN YOUR CAR TRUNK WITHOUT AN EXHAUST EXTENSION RISING ABOVE THE CAR-TOP TO DISCHARGE SAFELY THE CARBON MONOXIDE FUMES! DOGS BREATHING THIS GAS ENROUTE TO HUNT HAVE THEIR SENSES AND ENERGY REDUCED BELOW PAR.

RIGHT

FREE OF FUMES

**F**LEXIBLE EXHAUST TUBING TO EXTEND 1 FT. ABOVE CAR-TOP IS ATTACHED WITH CLAMPS AND SUCTION CUPS. WHEN UNUSED, REMOVE.

# DOG EXTRAS FOR A HUNTING SEASON

**Chapter 8**

**Your Dog**

The average dog travels 50 or more miles per day when hunting. Therefore he needs extra food and ¼ pound of suet or fat for this extra energy.

Dogs should always be exercised daily for two or three weeks before season starts, climaxed by a few vigorous workouts. If that is impossible, do not overwork the dog the first few times in hunting. Rest a dog now and then during the day. It's good for _you_, too!

His legs pick up fewer burs if extra hair is trimmed off.

# DOG BOOTS FOR ROUGH TERRAIN!

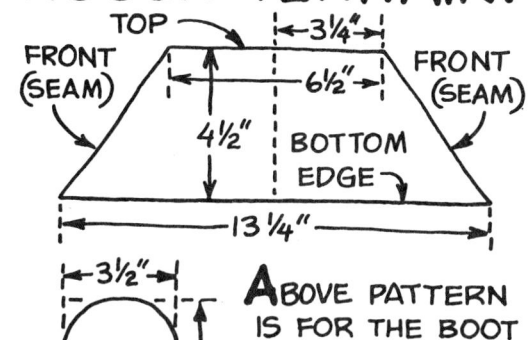

Chapter 8
Your Dog

ABOVE PATTERN IS FOR THE BOOT SIDE. IT CAN BE MADE OF 8 OZ. DUCK CLOTH OR BED TICKING. THE SOLE IS 16 OR 18 OZ. DUCK CLOTH. SOLE'S CIRCUMFERENCE VARIES WITH EACH MAKER. THUS, THE BOOT TOP DIMENSIONS ARE APPROXIMATE. CUT THE FIRST BOOT PIECES FROM OLD CLOTH, MAKING PAPER TRACINGS OF EACH BEFORE SEWING FOR LATER COPIES IF THE FIRST FITS. DOG SIZE DETERMINES BOOT SIZE. BOOTS MUST BE EXTRA LARGE FOR FOOT ACTION. SEW TOGETHER INSIDE OUT, BOTTOM EDGE TO SOLE, THEN FRONT SEAM. WIND TAPE TO LEG

# RAIN DESTROYS THE SCENT FOR DOGS

Chapter 8

Your Dog

Don't blame your dog when game is difficult to find or trail during rainy weather. First, most game birds may be sitting tight under clumps of heavy weeds or protecting trees out of the wet. Motionless birds give off little or no scent. Second, rain quickly washes away all track or trail scent.

# USING A BELL FOR YOUR HUNTING DOG

Chapter 8

Your Dog

WHERE BIRD DOGS ARE USED IN HEAVY, BROKEN COVER, A SMALL SHEEP BELL WORN ON THE COLLAR IS AN ADVANTAGE. SOME HUNTERS BELIEVE THE SOUND MAKES THE BIRDS FLUSH WILD BUT BELLED-DOG OWNERS CLAIM THAT BIRDS SIT TIGHTER BECAUSE THEY ARE CURIOUS ABOUT THE UNUSUAL RINGING.

A HUNTER KNOWS WHERE THE DOG IS WHEN HE CAN'T SEE HIM. QUIETNESS USUALLY MEANS HE IS HOLDING POINT ON GAME. A DOG GETS USED TO THE SOUND.

# HOW TO REMOVE BURS WITH LESS TROUBLE!

**Chapter 8**

**Your Dog**

The fall season's cockleburs, weed lice stickers, etc., usually cause the dog's master many dreary hours of work removing them painlessly from a sensitive dog's ears, legs, tail, etc. You can make this work much less tiring <u>if before going afield</u> with your dog you rub <u>white vasoline</u> on the most difficult areas!

# HOW TO RID YOUR DOG OF TICKS......

**Chapter 8**

**Your Dog**

Mix one ounce of soap and two ounces of derris powder (containing four percent rotenone) in one gallon of water. Wash your dog with this dip <u>BUT</u> <u>DO NOT</u> let it get into the dog's eyes! Let it dry on the dog's coat.

This treatment twice a week will do the trick in tick infested regions!

# PORCUPINE QUILLS REMOVED EASILY...

**Chapter 8**

**Your Dog**

Thanks to Frank J. Simpson, 16131 S.E. Mc Laughlin Blvd., Milwaukee Oregon, who sent this to us.

Frank says, "Pour a few spoonfuls of acid vinegar on the quills; then repeat in 5 or 10 minutes. Wait a few minutes, then pour any kind of oil over the quills and watch results. The acid removes the lime from the quills and they simply soften or wilt and after the oil is applied the quills simply pop out without touching."

He says it's painless, having used it with perfect results!

# SKUNKS VS. DOGS

They will meet and the skunk never comes out second best but dogs do not know this, so if possible, keep YOUR dog away from them.

If the worst does happen to your dog, the best remedy is wash him well with cans of tomatoes or tomato juice. Rub it into the hair and skin, and if IT affects the eyes, bathe them also.

All wild animals respect the skunk's weapon!

Chapter 8

Your Dog

**Chapter 8**

**Your Dog**

# HOW TO CLEANSE A DOG'S EARS.......

HOLD STICK PARALLEL TO DOG'S HEAD

**D**O NOT MAKE THE COMMON MISTAKE OF USING A ROUGH WASH CLOTH WITH SOAP AND WATER.

**W**RAP A BIT OF COTTON AROUND THE TIP OF A SMALL STICK AND DIP THIS SWAB IN OLIVE OIL OR PEROXIDE. HOLD THE EAR FLAP BACK AND CARE- FULLY CLEAN THE INSIDE. DO NOT GO DEEPER THAN YOU CAN SEE. DON'T JAB AND YOUR DOG WON'T HINDER THE WORK BY FLINCHING.

# USEFUL DOG TIPS

Here is an easy method of weighing a frisky dog on bathroom scales!

Weigh yourself and the dog together. Then put the dog down and weigh yourself. Subtract your weight from the first reading to find the dog's weight!

Don't tie a dog on a leash in a car by an open window. He could strangle himself if he decided to jump out!

Chapter 8

Your Dog

# PREPARING AND COOKING GAME

Generally speaking, the manner in which game is killed and dressed has a great effect upon the flavor. A clean, instant killing is no doubt the best. An animal that is wounded before the kill usually doesn't taste its best.

Cooking varies as much as do individual cooks. Some sportsmen go to considerable effort to prepare and cook their game while others do it the **easiest** way without regard to the outcome. Nearly all game makes fine **eating** when properly cared for, and **gourmets** place game high on the list of choice meats. However, do not think for a minute that game recipes need be complicated for tasty results. On the contrary, a simple recipe may prove the best for some species. Just try cooking **young** rabbits the same way you would a frying chicken. A lot of home **recipes work** very well for game. Venison **steak** can be cooked like veal or beef.

The married man is lucky if his wife is interested in going with him to his hunting camp. She'll be sure to have something to say about the cooking, even though a cook may be employed by the packer, outfitter or guide. If you're without a regular cook, she'll be a Godsend if she takes over the cooking so the hunters can rest after a strenuous day. At the same time, if she decides to have a try at this hunting business — from then on she won't let you leave without her when you hit for camp.

There are times when dehydrated foods are essential to the hiker, as on a pack trip when light weight is essential. But for the average modern camper using motor transportation generally, the regular canned foods are no handicap. Remember, it's always wise to take fresh meat or meat substitutes if you can, because you can't always depend upon game.

# FREEZER TIPS FOR BIRDS, WATERFOWL AND SMALL GAME

Chapter 9

Preparing and Cooking Game

**W**RAP THE GIBLETS IN A SEPARATE SMALL PACKAGE. SEAL WITH TAPE AND PLACE WITHIN THE BODY CAVITY. THUS, SHOULD THEY SPOIL, THE BIRD OR GAME WON'T BE AFFECTED.

BIRD IN BAG

VACUUM TUBE

**A**LL BIRDS MUST BE PLUCKED, NOT SKINNED. SKINNED BIRDS DRY OUT FASTER. UNPLUCKED FEATHERS TRAP UNWANTED AIR IN STORED PACKAGE. BUT, SMALL GAME MUST BE SKINNED. DRAW OUT THE SPOILING INNARDS.

**P**LASTIC FREEZER BAGS ARE IDEAL TO PACK A WHOLE BIRD OR GAME. PRESS OUT ALL AIR OR USE A VACUUM CLEANER TUBE TO DRAW IT OUT. TWIST AND FOLD BAG TOP. SECURE WITH RUBBER BAND.

# ELIMINATING "WILD TASTE" (SMALL GAME)

WOOD-CHUCK

SMALL SACKS OR KERNELS (GLANDS) THAT ARE FOUND ON THE INSIDE OF THE FRONT AND HIND LEGS AND SOMETIMES ELSEWHERE (AS ON A WOODCHUCK'S BACK) SHOULD BE REMOVED WHEN ANIMAL IS SKINNED. THE WHITE TO BROWNISH OBLONG GLANDS ARE LOCATED JUST UNDER THE SKIN, USUALLY IN THE FAT WHICH SHOULD ALWAYS BE REMOVED.

SOAK GAMEY MEAT IN SALT WATER OVERNIGHT. THEN, RECOVER MEAT IN COLD WATER. ADD A LEVEL TABLESPOON OF BLACK PEPPER AND ONE OF BAKING SODA. SLOWLY BRING TO A BOIL. POUR OFF LIQUID. RINSE MEAT, THEN REPEAT AGAIN. RECOVER WITH COLD WATER, PARBOIL BEFORE FRYING OR ROASTING. OR, SEASON AND STEW UNTIL TENDER.

Chapter 9

Preparing and Cooking Game

**Chapter 9**

**Preparing and Cooking Game**

# PROPER "AGING" OF GAME MEAT

Storage of BIG GAME for several days below 50° F. temperature ages or cures it. Meat tissue breaks down and becomes more tender while aging, but it shrinks in weight as it becomes drier. Less fatty game such as a young buck antelope requires very little if any aging.

PRONGHORN ANTELOPE

Tough old bears should age two weeks or more at 35° to 40°; young ones, a day or two less.

Age moose about like bear.

Elk may be aged from two to ten days. Deer a few days longer. Freezing cold will stop the aging process.

# TIP FOR BETTER FLAVORED RABBITS!

As soon as you shoot a rabbit, remove its entrails neatly by slitting the abdominal cavity from the rib cage to the tail as shown by the dotted line. Grasp the rabbit's front and hind legs with its belly down. A quick circular snap outward sends the innards flying. Their quick removal insures fresher flavor.

**Chapter 9**

Preparing and Cooking Game

# FRIED COTTONTAIL RABBIT!

**Chapter 9**

Preparing and Cooking Game

Soak a cleaned rabbit in salt and vinegar water for 8 or 10 hrs. Then cut into pieces. Sprinkle with flour, salt and pepper. Dip pieces in a beaten mixture of 1 egg and 1/4 cup of milk then roll each piece in cracker or bread crumbs. Heat in a skillet 1/4 cup of lard or shortening until very hot. Brown rabbit on both sides. Add 1/2 cup water. Cover and cook in a 325° oven until tender. Remove pieces and make a gravy with the drippings! Good!

# TRY HUNTERS' PIE

**Chapter 9**

**Preparing and Cooking Game**

Cut 1 rabbit or 2 squirrels into pieces. Place in a pan and barely cover with water. Cover pan to simmer until tender. Add salt while it cooks. Drain and measure the liquid. Bone the meat. Heat 3 tbsp. butter in a skillet. Add 2 tbsp. chopped onion and 2 tbsp. chopped parsley. Adding 1½ tbsp. flour for each measured cup of liquid, stir as it cooks 4 min. Add liquid, stirring until thick. Mix with boned meat in bake dish. Cover with pie crust. Bake brown.

# QUAIL ON TOAST

MALE BOBWHITE QUAIL

Chapter 9

Preparing and Cooking Game

Pluck and clean birds. Rub butter, salt and pepper on the inside and out. Lay strips of bacon on the breast, binding in wings and legs. Place in roaster having one tablespoon of butter and two of water for each bird. Cook until done in hot oven, basting frequently. Remove birds from pan. Place each on a hot slice of buttered toast. Add a little butter, water and one lemon's juice to the pan. Simmer for three minutes then pour over quail on toast. Garnish with parsley and serve while hot.

# FRIED PHEASANT IS GOOD EATING!

Chapter 9

Preparing and Cooking Game

Cut into pieces as you would a frying chicken. Salt and pepper and roll each piece in flour. Brown well on all sides in equal parts of butter and shortening. Add a little water to the skillet and cover to simmer. Test with a fork frequently until it is tender.

Make gravy by using the drippings left in the skillet. Sound good? It is!

Keep it simple. The true flavor is often lost by using too many ingredients.

# WATERFOWL PICKING TIP FOR QUICK JOB

Chapter 9

Preparing and Cooking Game

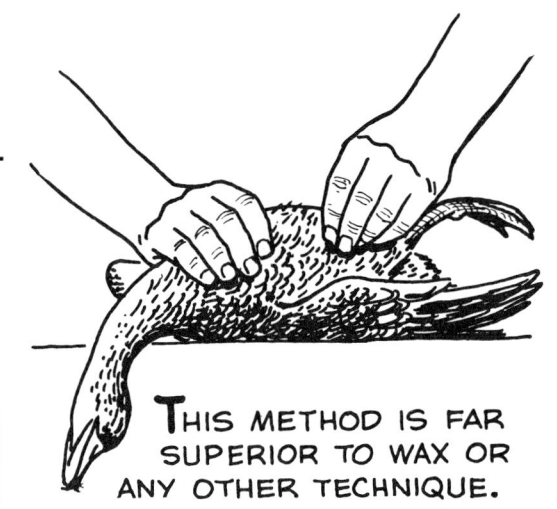

This method is far superior to wax or any other technique.

Mix two tablespoons of household <u>DETERGENT</u> (same as used in washing dishes, sold in all grocery markets) into a large, two or three gallon bucket of boiling water. Remove water from stove. Hold bird by its head and submerge its body into the hot solution for one minute. Use something to force body under if needed. Rinse in cold, running water then pick feathers and down.

# COOKING TIPS ON WATERFOWL........

Canadian Geese

**Chapter 9**

Preparing and Cooking Game

All wild geese are drier than domestic species when roasted because they have less fat. Therefore place a wild goose breast down in the roasting pan and lay slices of bacon to cover the back. Use a moist dressing for the stuffing.

Baste about every 5 minutes with a warm mixture of melted butter (1/8 th lb.), 1/2 cup of lemon juice, 2 tablespoons of catsup, 1/2 teaspoon of prepared mustard, 1 teaspoon of Worcestershire sauce, salt and pepper.

Chapter 9

Preparing and Cooking Game

# BUTCHERING DEER

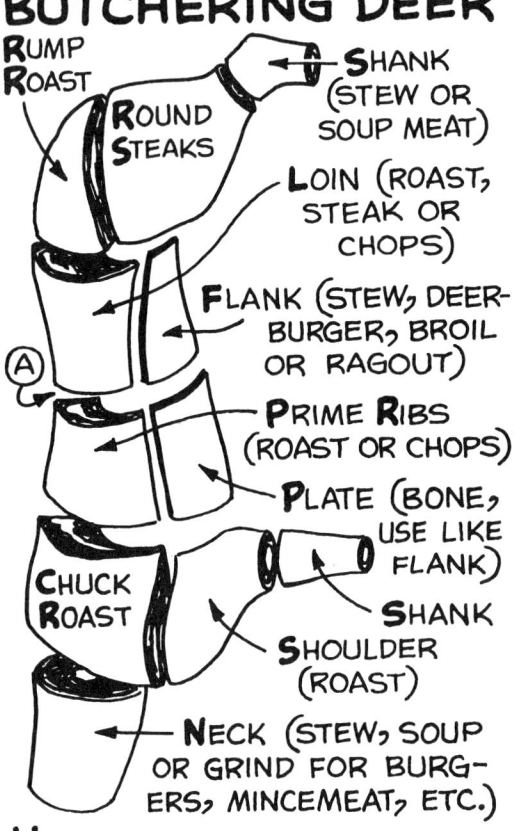

- **R**ump **R**oast
- **R**ound **S**teaks
- **S**hank (stew or soup meat)
- **L**oin (roast, steak or chops)
- **F**lank (stew, deerburger, broil or ragout)
- **P**rime **R**ibs (roast or chops)
- **P**late (bone, use like flank)
- **C**huck **R**oast
- **S**hank
- **S**houlder (roast)
- **N**eck (stew, soup or grind for burgers, mincemeat, etc.)

Hang carcass and saw in half, lengthwise from tail down through backbone and neck. Cut each half as above. Divide hind and forequarter by cutting between 1st and 2nd ribs (A) with a knife and a saw for the bone.

# -ROAST VENISON-

The meat on the back over the ribs is called the saddle. Cut a roast of...

Chapter 9

Preparing and Cooking Game

...this and marinate it in a mixture

A MULE DEER

of 1⅓ cupfuls of red wine, ⅔ cup of water, a bit of pepper, bay leaves, thyme, mustard seed and a sliced onion. Soak 24 hours, turn occasionally. Stick a few slivers of garlic in the meat and salt it. Roast in a 350° oven, basting with marinate mix and meat drippings. Remove meat when done. Add ½ cup sour cream, 1 glass of currant jelly and 1 tablespoon of brandy to the gravy. Stir over a high flame until it thickens.

# LATE SEASON TIPS FOR TASTY VENISON

**Chapter 9**

Preparing and Cooking Game

Where game laws regulate keeping venison beyond the initial period by securing a special permit, with luck, you may still have some. Aging venison sometimes loses its best flavor and dries out in the freezer. Venison, as with other game, is best when fresh from the oven, broiler or pot.

Roast left-overs make tasty stews. Prepare with the usual vegetables, salt, pepper, gravy. Or lacking that, thicken with flour paste. Cook slowly.

Fat should always be removed before cooking venison. Use bacon fat or other fats instead.

# IS RED THE SAFEST COLOR FOR HUNTING?

**Chapter 10**

**Woodcraft for the Hunter**

For many years red has been recognized as the safest color and in some areas, it is the law today. At a distance, some dark reds in shadowed cover appear to be brown. The new LUMINOUS LIGHT reds and yellows have great visibility.

The American Optometric Association says red isn't recognizable to the color blind whereas large black and white or colored checks are recognized by all and so are safer!

BANDANA -- WESTERN STYLE.

221

# COMPASS TRICKS..

**Chapter 10**

Woodcraft for the Hunter

AN OUT-
DOORSMAN
SHOULD
REMOVE
METALIC
GEAR...

...SUCH AS A GUN, KNIFE, AXE, ETC., TO SEVERAL FEET AWAY WHEN TAKING A COMPASS READING. EVEN HOLDING A COMPASS CLOSE TO A BELT BUCKLE MAY AFFECT ITS ACCURACY! STAY AWAY FROM RAILWAY TRACKS, IRON BRIDGES, ETC.

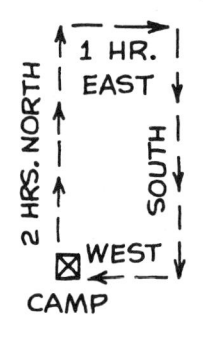

INSTEAD OF COUNTING YOUR PACES TO A MILE, USE YOUR WATCH TO MEASURE. MAINTAIN A STEADY PACE. IF YOU "MOSEY" ALONG IN HUNTING, DON'T SPEED UP LATER.

# LOCATING NORTH WITHOUT A COMPASS

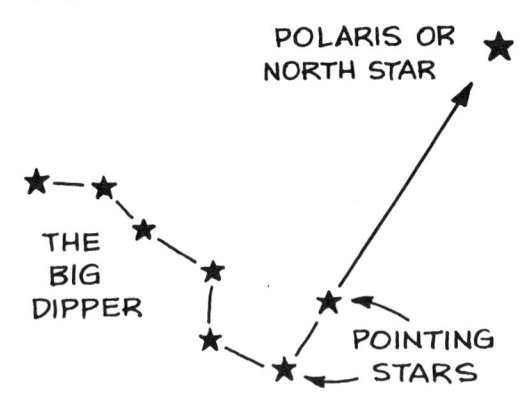

POLARIS OR NORTH STAR

THE BIG DIPPER

POINTING STARS

Chapter 10

Woodcraft for the Hunter

The north star is located almost directly above the north pole (the earth's axis). If you should become lost without a compass you can always locate this star by finding the big dipper first. The dipper's two end stars are the pointers. They line up with the north star.

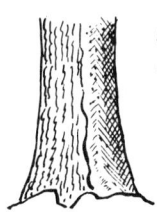

Moss may be found growing on the north side of some tree trunks.

Foliage is heavier on the SOUTH side on most trees.

Chapter 10

Woodcraft for the Hunter

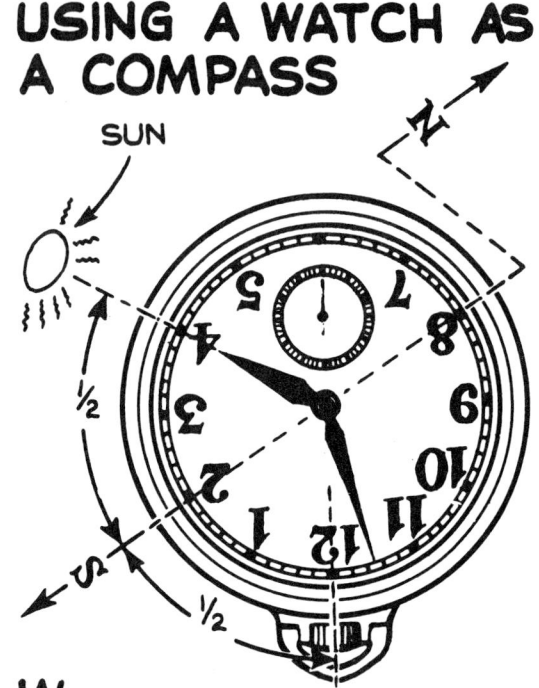

## USING A WATCH AS A COMPASS

Without a compass you may substitute a watch by holding it face-up and pointing the hour or small hand directly at the sun. One-half the distance between the hour hand and twelve o'clock will be due south.

Direction should be established upon entering areas and reversed coming out.

# MARKING A TRAIL

TRAIL IS THIS WAY →

Chapter 10

Woodcraft for the Hunter

Where tree-blazing a trail is illegal, bushes or brush may be used instead to mark a trail. Break or cut almost through, near the base, to lean the bush on the ground pointing the direction you take. It helps to relocate cached game, find camp or trail out.

Don't depend upon backtracking yourself when in strange surroundings, even in snow where others' tracks may confuse you or new snow may cover.

Rock on a rock means, "The Trail".

This means, "Turn, Follow Point".

**Chapter 10**

**Woodcraft for the Hunter**

# "LINING OUT" AVOIDS WALKING IN CIRCLES

You can "line out" through the woods without getting off your course by...

...lining up three or four trees in a straight line and before passing the remaining two trees, pick another up ahead that lines up with them.

You'll hike out in a straight line and not be wandering in circles.

# DISTRESS SIGNALS EVERYONE SHOULD KNOW!

Chapter 10

Woodcraft for the Hunter

If you have never been lost, you cannot know the desperate helplessness that may overcome you!

The universal signal for help or "I'm lost" is three shots fired in succession. Wait a bit and fire three more etc. Two quick shots is the proper acknowledged reply.

Three smoke columns mean the same thing. Two columns acknowledge.

# SURVIVOR'S TIPS!

**Chapter 10**

Woodcraft for the Hunter

Chances for air rescue are good if: you're near a traveled air route; weather and observation are good; you don't get excited when you realize you are lost; your companions notify nearest forest ranger, police or civil air patrol; you stay in open and on ridges where you are easily seen.

Chances are poor if: you're off traveled air lanes; visibility from the air is poor; you stay in wooded areas, ravines, so you can't be seen; your companions don't notify law officers; you start to wander.

Signal aircraft with 3 fires 100 ft. apart or mirror.

# EMERGENCY SHELTER

**Chapter 10**

**Woodcraft for the Hunter**

A BRUSH LEAN-TO CAN BE MADE WITH A BELT AXE OR WITHOUT ONE IF SMALL, BREAKABLE BRUSH IS HANDY. IT WILL NOT SHED RAIN BUT IT CAN HELP TURN WIND AND SNOW. EVERGREEN BOUGHS WOVEN TIGHTLY INTO THE FRAME WORKS BETTER THAN BRUSH.

OVERLAP BOUGHS FROM BOTTOM TO TOP.

QUARTER ROUND STRIPS OF LOOSE BARK OVERLAPPED LIKE SHINGLES AND WEIGHTED DOWN WILL TURN RAIN.

# PURIFYING YOUR DRINKING WATER...

**Chapter 10**

**Woodcraft for the Hunter**

WILDERNESS STREAMS AND LAKES USUALLY OFFER THE PUREST WATER. DISCOLORED WATER MAY BE FILTERED TO CLEAR IT AND BOILED FOR 15 MINUTES TO PURIFY IT AND THEN COOLED FOR DRINKING. ONE-HALF TEASPOON OF FRESH CHLORIDE OF LIME IN A PINT OF <u>ANY</u> WATER WILL PURIFY IT. AS A RULE, THE FARTHER THE WATER IS FROM HUMAN HABITATION, THE SAFER IT IS!

# QUICKSAND "KNOW-HOW" PROTECTION!

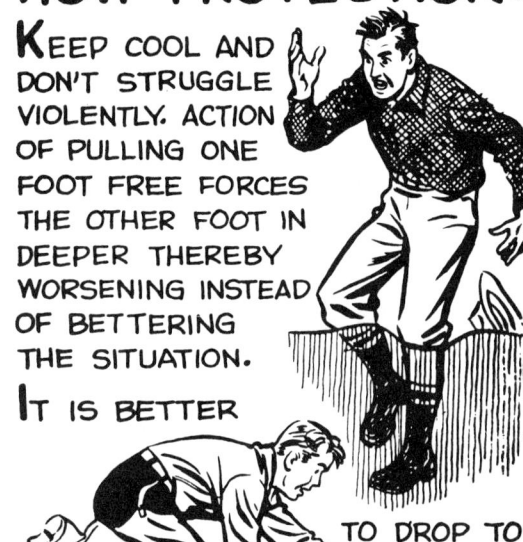

KEEP COOL AND DON'T STRUGGLE VIOLENTLY. ACTION OF PULLING ONE FOOT FREE FORCES THE OTHER FOOT IN DEEPER THEREBY WORSENING INSTEAD OF BETTERING THE SITUATION.

IT IS BETTER TO DROP TO YOUR HANDS AND KNEES AND ATTEMPT TO CRAWL BECAUSE YOUR WEIGHT IS THEN DISTRIBUTED OVER A WIDER AREA. IF THE MIRE IS TOO SOFT FOR THAT, LIE FLAT ON YOUR STOMACH, MOVING ONLY A PART OF THE BODY AT ONE TIME. FLOAT IF YOU KNOW HOW, THE <u>WATER</u> IS BUOYANT.

Chapter 10

Woodcraft for the Hunter

# AN IDEAL CAMPSITE

**Chapter 10**

Woodcraft for the Hunter

A BREEZY MOSQUITO-FREE SPOT THAT IS NEAR DRINKING WATER AND FIRE-WOOD. THE TENT SHOULD BE LOCATED ON A SLOPE FOR DRAINAGE (YOU MAY ALSO DIG A SMALL TRENCH, DEEPEST ON THE LOW OUTLET SIDE FOR ADDED PROTECTION). PROTECT AGAINST SUMMER'S MIDAFTERNOON SUN BY SHADE BUT BEWARE OF POSSIBLE FALLING TREE LIMBS. AVOID DEEP GRASS THAT MAY HARBOR TICKS, ETC.

# DON'T CAMP UPON YOUR HUNTING SITE!

Chapter 10

Woodcraft for the Hunter

BIG GAME HUNTING GUIDES AND OUTFITTERS WILL NOT SET UP CAMP HEADQUARTERS WITHIN THREE MILES OF THE AREA THEY EXPECT TO HUNT. A CAMP SMELLS OF COOKING, TOBACCO AND WOOD SMOKE, BESIDES THE HUMANS THEMSELVES. WIND WILL CARRY THESE ODORS, WARNING THE WARY GAME TO MOVE ON. LIKEWISE DO NOT BE OVERLY NOISY IN CHOPPING WOOD, ETC.

**Chapter 10**

**Woodcraft for the Hunter**

# TENT CAMP TIPS...

Don't pitch a tent under a lone, tall tree in a clearing...

...that might attract lightning in a storm!

Don't camp where aged or dead trees or limbs may fall from a wind. Smaller young trees offer shade and wind protection, are less likely to fall from wind or be hit by lightning.

A duck tent that shrinks when wet should have its guy ropes loosened when it rains so pegs don't pull out.

# CANVAS COVERING

Chapter 10

Woodcraft for the Hunter

Thanks to Norman S. Werry of the Gary, Indiana, Post-Tribune for this tip.

Include a light piece of canvas about 4' x 6' in your camp duffel. Use it as (1) a cover for gear when caught in a rain on open waters. (2) An emergency water "bucket". (3) A wood, etc. cover at night in case of rain. (4) A spread under your sleeping bag to block ground dampness. (5) A "table", spread for meals.

Other uses might include: outer cover for pack-horse rig; to set up to deflect wind from a cooking fire and to cover dressed big game against weather.

**Chapter 10**

**Woodcraft for the Hunter**

# PREVENTING FIRES!

Always break a burned match in the middle before throwing it away. By so doing you're making sure it's out!

Don't smoke in forbidden areas of forests or away from camp when the woods are tinder dry!

Clear the ground for several feet around your campfire BEFORE you build one. Keep your fire small and under control at all times and do not leave it unattended at any time!

Put water and or dirt on a fire whenever leaving camp.

# BE CAREFUL WITH CAMPFIRES!

**Chapter 10**

Woodcraft for the Hunter

Don't build a fire against ANY tree or stump! After you think it's put out when you leave, ROOTS, leading to other trees' roots, may smolder for hours UNDERGROUND before starting a new fire!

Use wood that won't throw popping sparks out to ignite nearby brush or leaves.

Don't leave fire burning at night when going to bed. It could spread from winds.

Douse all untended fires!

Chapter 10

Woodcraft for the Hunter

# A CAMP FIRE TIP...

BREEZE

Thanks to MR. L.W. LACEKY OF GUNNISON, COLORADO, WHO SENT IT TO US!

Lay two logs of equal diameter about a foot apart and parallel. Build a fire between them. When it burns down to red hot coals roll the logs close enough to set pots and pans along the top. It's a good cooking surface and the fire can be strung out between logs for more utensils. If logs are green they may be used to cook several meals on. Try to place logs so the most constant breezes go between them.

# CAMPFIRE USES OF FORKED STICKS

One of the most popular campfire uses is shown here. Short, pot-holding forks are notched for pot's bail to cook at varied heights.

Always use green sticks near fires.

A 'dinglestick' has a fork or notch to hold the pot. A heavy rock may be used to hold the end down instead of the fork shown.

Chapter 10

Woodcraft for the Hunter

**Chapter 10**

Woodcraft for the Hunter

# QUICK CAMPFIRES

Natural starters are: birch bark, pine knots and <u>dry</u> pine cones, cedar shavings, palmetto fans, grapevine bark, cactus spines and dead limbs. These make some of the best tinder even after a rain.

Dry kindling is added next. Use split pine, cedar, juniper, pinon, balsam, chestnut, spruce, hemlock, etc.

Low hanging dead limbs may be knocked from a live tree. These will be comparatively dry after a rain. Any wet bark may be easily shaved away.

Don't use kerosene to start a cook fire as it may taste.

# CAMPFIRE TRICKS

The shaved stick is an old stand-by that ignites quickly. Slow-burning wood starts quicker if smaller kindling is shaved with a knife first.

Chapter 10

Woodcraft for the Hunter

If you want a quick, hot fire to heat or cook with, split the wood into small pieces.

← PULL TIGHT →

Here is a starter that burns enough to start small damp sticks. Wrap wool yarn the length of a kitchen match and tie off as shown. Dip full length in parafin. Chip off the tip to strike. Pack in a tobacco can for future use.

Dry pine needles found in hollow logs are good fire starters in wet weather.

# HOW TO SLEEP WARM IN CAMP!

**Chapter 10**

Woodcraft for the Hunter

When sleeping on the ground in cold weather, build a fire where you intend to sleep. Put some large stones in the fire to heat them through. When ready to retire, scrape the fire to one side and bury the stones just under the surface of warmed earth. It will aid comfort to shape shallows to fit your hips and shoulders in the earth. Use a ground cloth under your bedding. More stones may be left to heat in a fire as you sleep in case you need to remake bed during the night.

A canteen filled with boiling water makes a good foot warmer. Change to dry garments before retiring.

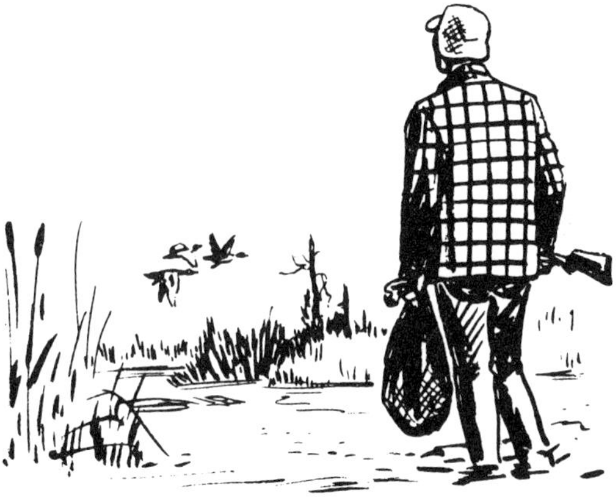

# INDEX

Ammunition, 159-161, 177
Animal lure, 98

Bags for hunters, 71
Bears, 72
Beavers, 101
Binoculars, 181-185
Blinds, 33-38, 50
Bobcats, 74-76
Boots, 178, 187
Bullets, 159-161

Caliber, 160; also see Rifles
Camps, 232-242
Campfires, 236-240
Carriers, 86-88, 191
Clothing, 178, 187-189, 221
Compass, 222-224
Cooking, 206-220, 238
Coons, 21, 99-100, 112
Crows, 30-32

Decoys, 40-43
Deer, 52-71, 77-78, 82, 84-91, 218-220
Distress signals, 227-228

Dogs, 192-205
Doves, 9
Drop, 168-170
Ducks, 9, 33-49
Duck calls, 44

Equipment and its care, 171-191

Field care of game birds, 29
Field care of deer, 69-70
Fires, 236-240
Forward allowance, 66, 153-155
Foxes, 9, 106-109

Geese, 9, 50, 217
Grouse, 9, 25-26
Gun care, 121, 132-133, 142, 156-158, 163, 173-176, 180; also see Marksmanship, Rifles, Shotguns
Gun covers, 176

Hanging big game, 82-83, 89-90

Jump shooting, 48

Knives, 179, 186

Lamps, 39, 179
Lead allowance, 66, 153-155
Lubricants, 174-175

Marksmanship, 121, 128-155
Mattresses, 178
Muskrats, 94-97

Offhand shots, 128
Opossums, 105, 112
Outdoor gear, 178-179

Partridge, 25-26
Pheasants, 9, 27-28, 215
Pitch, 168-170
"Pointing" out, 152
Possums, 105, 112

Quail, 9, 23-24, 214
Quicksand, 231

Rabbits, 9-16, 211-213
Raccoons, 21, 99-100, 112
Recoil, 139-141
Rifles, 131-135, 138-139, 141-143, 156-162, 164-165, 173; also see Gun care, Marksmanship

Safety, 49, 122-127, 144
Sheep, bighorn, 73
Shelter, emergency, 229
Shooting range, estimating, 45-47
Shotguns, 139, 156-157, 164-170; also see Gun care, Marksmanship
Sights, 131-133, 164-165, 180
Skinning, 79, 113-115
Skunks, 105, 112, 203
Sleeping bags, 178
Snap shooting, 151, 155
Snipe, 9
Squirrels, 9, 17-20, 113, 213
Stalking, 22, 59-60
"Stand," 39, 56-57, 74
Stoves, 39, 179

Tanning, 116-120
Target practice, 135-136, 144-149
Tents, 178, 190, 232-234
Tracks, 63-65
Trails, marking, 225
Trapping, 92-112
Trophies, 77-78, 82, 84
Turkeys, 9

Venison, 218-220

Water, purifying, 230

Weasels, 102-105
Wing shooting, 148-150
Woodcock, 9

## EVERYDAY HANDBOOKS (Continued)

Everyday Handbooks (#201-300) are self-teaching books on academic subjects, skills, and hobbies. The majority of these books sell for $1.25 to $2.25. Many are available in cloth bindings at a higher price.

### PHILOSOPHY, RELIGION

IDEAS OF THE GREAT PHILOSOPHERS, 218
OUTLINE OF THE BIBLE, Book by Book, 263
RELIGION IN THE UNITED STATES, 294
RELIGIONS OF THE WORLD, 224

### PSYCHOLOGY, SOCIOLOGY

DR. FROMME'S BOOK ON SEX AND MARRIAGE, 264
LAYMAN'S DICTIONARY OF PSYCHIATRY, 211
LAYMAN'S GUIDE TO PSYCHIATRY, 220
MODERN PSYCHOLOGY, 231
SOCIOLOGY: An Introduction to the Science of Society, 268

### SCIENCE

BIOLOGY FOR THE MODERN WORLD, 288
ELECTRONICS IN EVERYDAY THINGS, 291
FOSSILS: An Introduction to Prehistoric Life, 280
FUNDAMENTALS OF PHYSIOLOGY, 221
MAKING FRIENDS WITH THE STARS, 227
PHYSICS FOR THE MODERN WORLD, 290
ROCKS AND MINERALS, 260

### CRAFTS, GAMES

ANTIQUES FOR AMATEURS, 243
ART COLLECTING FOR AMATEURS, 234
ATTACK AND COUNTERATTACK IN CHESS, 204

### CRAFTS, GAMES (Continued)

BODY-BUILDING AND SELF-DEFENSE, 258
CHESS FOR BEGINNERS: A Picture Guide, 223
CHESS SELF-TEACHER, 257
COMPLETE BOOK OF CHESS OPENINGS, 274
ETIQUETTE FOR TODAY, 272
FIRST BOOK OF BRIDGE, 242
FIRST BOOK OF CHESS, 241
HOW TO BUILD A COIN COLLECTION, 208
HOW TO DANCE, 202
HOW TO DRAW AND PAINT, 244
HOW TO WIN CHESS GAMES QUICKLY, 269
IMPROVING YOUR CHESS, 267
MODERN SKIING, 222
PARTY GAMES, 216
SILVER COLLECTING FOR AMATEURS, 250
SPORTSMAN'S DIGEST OF FISHING, 247
SPORTSMAN'S DIGEST OF HUNTING, 248
WATSON'S CLASSIC BOOK ON THE PLAY OF THE HAND AT BRIDGE, 209
YOUR GUIDE TO BOATING, 238
YOUR GUIDE TO PHOTOGRAPHY, 285

### STUDY AIDS

HOW TO IMPROVE YOUR MEMORY, 273
NOTESCRIPT, 232
TESTMANSHIP: Seven Ways to Raise Your Examination Grades, 296
THINKING WITH A PENCIL, 206